7/17/74

REZNIKOFF, Charles. By the well of living & seeing; new & selected poems, 1918–1973, ed. with an intro. by Seamus Cooney. Black Sparrow, 1974. 173p 74-9559. 15.00, ISBN 0-87685-182-0; 4.00 pa. ISBN 0-87685-181-2. C.I.P.

Language & Literature

English & American

Now in his early 80s, Reznikoff came of poetic age at the time of the Imagist movement, and his work — with its lack of softly descriptive language and its preference for free verse and straightforward language — shows clear marks still of the ancient credo. At times the plainness of language slips perilously close to uninteresting prose, but at his best, Reznikoff is a curiously moving poet. Perhaps a certain moral insight and intensity fuse with the simplicity of language to produce a sense of a real human being writing about real men and women. He can be powerfully laconic, as in describing the beginning of an affair, "Their new landlord was a handsome man. On his rounds to collect rent she became friendly. / Finally, she asked him in to have a cup of tea. After that he came often." He has a very strong sense of history, American and Jewish both, and deeply identifies himself with the bittersweet pageant of Jewish existence. All in all, this book is more impressive than the sum of its parts. The totality is not just a poetic experience, but acquaintance with a beautiful soul.

163

Reznikoff, Charles. By the Well of Living & Seeing: new & selected poems, 1918-1973.

Black Sparrow. 1974. 173p. ed. & intro. by Seamus Cooney. LC 74-9559. pap. $4; signed cloth ed. $15.   POETRY

This comprehensive selection (which includes a valuable introduction and textual notes) belongs in every college library. Reznikoff, who deserves a wider reading than he has received, alternates between tightly crafted objectivist glimpses of urban landscapes and more expansive, emotionally open Whitman-esque vignettes of people going about their daily business. He tells a good story in verse, especially when the subject is Jewish history or heritage. Reznikoff's ethnic rootedness is rare in American poetry, as is his feel for New York City life. His voice has a resonant echo.—*Norbert Krapf, English Dept., C. W. Post Coll., Greenvale, N.Y.*

Also by CHARLES REZNIKOFF

Rhythms, 1918
Rhythms II, 1919
Poems, 1920
Uriel Accosta: A Play & A Fourth Group of Verse, 1921
Chatterton, The Black Death, and Meriwether Lewis, 1922 (plays)
Coral and Captive Israel, 1923 (plays)
Nine Plays, 1927
Five Groups of Verse, 1927
By the Waters of Manhattan, 1929 (anthology)
By the Waters of Manhattan, 1930 (novel)
Jerusalem the Golden, 1934
Testimony, 1934 (prose)
In Memoriam: 1933, 1934
Early History of a Sewing Machine Operator (with Nathan
    Reznikoff), 1936 (prose
Separate Way, 1936
Going To and Fro and Walking Up and Down, 1941
The Lionhearted, 1944 (novel)
Inscriptions: 1944-1956, 1959
By the Waters of Manhattan: Selected Verse, 1962
Family Chronicle (with Nathan and Sarah Reznikoff), 1963 (prose)
Testimony: The United States 1885-1890: Recitative, 1965
Testimony: The United States (1891-1900): Recitative, 1968
By the Well of Living and Seeing and The Fifth Book of the
    Maccabees, 1969

Charles Reznikoff

BY THE WELL
OF LIVING
&
SEEING
New & Selected
Poems 1918-1973

Edited with an Introduction
by
Seamus Cooney

BLACK SPARROW PRESS / LOS ANGELES / 1974

ACKNOWLEDGEMENT

Some of the poems in this book first appeared in *Commentary*, *The Menorah Journal*, *Midstream*, and *Poetry*, to whose editors grateful acknowledgement is made, and in the books *Rhythms*, *Rhythms II, Poems, Urial Accosta: A Play & A Fourth Group of Verse, Five Groups of Verse, By the Waters of Manhattan: An Annual, Jerusalem the Golden, In Memoriam: 1933, Separate Way, Going To and Fro and Walking Up and Down, Inscriptions: 1944-1956*, and *By the Well of Living and Seeing and The Fifth Book of the Maccabees*, all published by Charles Reznikoff under various imprints.

The editor gratefully acknowledges receipt of a Faculty Research Fellowship from Western Michigan University in support of his work on this edition.

LIBRARY OF CONGRESS CATALOGING IN PUBLICATION DATA

Reznikoff, Charles, 1894-
  By the well of living and seeing.

  I. Title.
PS3535.E98B85   811'.5'2   74-9559
ISBN 0-87685-182-0
ISBN 0-87685-181-2 (pbk.)

to Marie:

Your beauty is like that of a tree whose beauty outlasts its flowers,
like that of a light constantly
losing its rays through the hours
and seasons, and still aglow
through twilight and darkness, through moths and snow.

TABLE OF CONTENTS

Introduction

From *Rhythms* (1918)

From *Rhythms II* (1919)

From *Poems* (1920)

From *Uriel Accosta: A Play & A Fourth Group of Verse* (1921)

From *Five Groups of Verse* (1927)

From "Editing and Glosses" in *By the Waters of Manhattan* (1929)

From *Jerusalem the Golden* (1934)

From *In Memoriam: 1933* (1934)

From *Separate Way* (1936)

From *Going To and Fro and Walking Up and Down* (1941)

Jews in Babylonia (uncollected, 1969)

From *Holocaust* (unpublished, 1973)

Textual Notes / 169

INTRODUCTION

Charles Reznikoff's biography—sketched briefly at the end of this volume—yields two or three critically relevant facts, helpful in directing attention to some of the salient qualities of his work. They are his date of birth (1894), his cultural ancestry (Jewish), and his almost uninterrupted residence in New York.

His date of birth places his literary coming of age at the height of the Imagist movement, and thus directs our attention to the enduring affinity his work has shown to the principles of that group. Not that a particular school monopolized his attention: he has spoken of his admiration in youth for work as diverse as that of John Millington Synge and Masters' *Spoon River Anthology* (1915).[1] Nevertheless, it was Ezra Pound, in those communications he sent to *Poetry* from his base in London, who most helpfully spelled out the principles which guided many young American writers, Reznikoff among them. So much so, indeed, that Reznikoff's fellow "Objectivist" Carl Rakosi has referred to Pound's celebrated "Don'ts for Imagists," which appeared in the March 1913 issue of *Poetry*, as "an absolute foundation stone of contemporary American writing."[2] The foundation stone is now so solidly incorporated into the edifice that I need only quote a few phrases to recall the gist. First the Imagist principles:

1. Direct treatment of the "thing," whether subjective or objective.
2. To use absolutely no word that did not contribute to the presentation.
3. As regarding rhythm: to compose in the sequence of the musical phrase, not in sequence of a metronome.

And from the "Don'ts":

Use no superfluous word. . . .

. . .the natural object is always the *adequate* symbol. . . .
Use either no ornament or good ornament.

Don't imagine that a thing will "go" in verse just because
it's too dull to go in prose.

Don't be "viewy"—leave that to the writers of pretty little
philosophic essays. Don't be descriptive; remember that the
painter can describe a landscape much better than you can. . . .

When Shakespeare talks of the "Dawn in russet mantle
clad" he presents something which the painter does not present.
There is in this line of his nothing that one can call description;
he presents.

Don't chop your stuff into separate iambs.[5]

These principles are implicit in Reznikoff's poetic practice from his
first book, which contained this poem:

> *I step into the fishy pool*
> *As if into a cool*
> *Vault.*
> *I, too, become*
> *Cold-blooded, dumb.*

to his most recent, more than fifty years later, which contained
this one:

THE OLD MAN

> *The fish has too many bones*
> *and the watermelon too many seeds.*

The plangent vowel music has been replaced by a drier, more
astringent sound, but the continuity of the procedures is clear
enough. And as for theorizing about his work (which he has rarely
indulged in), compare with Pound's injunctions the following brief
description of his own poetry that Reznikoff furnished to the editors
of *Contemporary Poetry*:

"Objectivist," images clear but the meaning not stated but suggested by the objective details and the music of the verse; words pithy and plain; without the artifice of regular meters; themes, chiefly Jewish, American, urban.[4]

Reznikoff's Jewishness and New York milieu, as this note indicates, affect primarily his subject matter. From very early in his published poems (see numbers 15 and 17 below), we find him escaping from subjectivism and self-centeredness and recording with sympathy and directness his insights into other lives. At moments, indeed, one almost wants the poems to give names and places for the incidents they so poignantly record, so vivid are the glimpses they afford. But the actors are anonymous, located among concrete realities which are specified only just enough to free the emotion or insight and make it act on us. There is no information for information's sake, rather a paring to essentials. Collectively, the host of characters and scenes we meet in reading Reznikoff amount to an impressionistic contribution to the social history of New York. And it is characteristic that we most often see victims, the poor or ignorant or suffering. Here Reznikoff's urban Americanism connects with his Jewishness and the traditional fellow-feeling of the Jew for other victimized groups. C.P. Snow, speaking of Reznikoff's Jewishness, remarked: "He conveys, as sharply as I have ever seen conveyed in any writing about New York, the feeling of the lonely soul in the great city."[5] In part this effect comes from the perspective of five thousand years of Jewish history which is in so many ways kept present to the reader of Reznikoff—not least, of course, by the poems (and plays) based on historical or Biblical sources. (These, too, begin early, with the 1929 *Uriel Accosta*.) As the book titles suggest, the Reznikoff observer, ostensibly detached and objective, is implicitly sympathetic, responsive, and aware of history: he is "going to and fro, walking up and down," making "inscriptions" or doing "editing and glosses" in a place "by the waters of Manhattan" (as it might be by the waters of Babylon), or "by the well of living and seeing"—the phrase catching the role exactly in its combination of subjective and objective? In Reznikoff, the Imagist method provides not only revelations of the quiddity of natural things, or the transience of life, but often a perspective through the surface of quotidian city life onto stretches of the past—drawing on a specifically Jewish sense of historical and racial continuity. The effect can be poignant or—as in the following—humorous:

GOD AND MESSENGER

This pavement barren
as the mountain
on which God spoke to Moses—
suddenly in the street
shining against my legs
the bumper of a motor car.

The significant addition to the Imagist program, in Reznikoff's brief self-description, is signalled by the term "Objectivist," and a word must now be said on what it portends. It has a definable historical meaning in pointing to a group of writers who used it of themselves and their work, but only a vague and relatively unimportant meaning as a description of the qualities of that work—even less than that contained in the term "Imagist."

Historically, the word in its literary application first occurred in the February 1931 issue of *Poetry*, which was edited by the twenty-seven year old Louis Zukofsky. Harriet Monroe, we now know, having invited Zukofsky to be guest editor (at Ezra Pound's instigation), insisted that he should have a label for the group of poets he gathered, and it was in response to this urging that Zukofsky headed his editorial comment: "Program: 'Objectivists' 1931" (then, and later in the book title, *An "Objectivist" Anthology*, scrupulous to retain the inverted commas around the term). As a heading to his piece, Zukofsky gave his definition:

An Objective: (Optics)—The lens bringing the rays from an object to a focus. (Military use)—That which is aimed at. (Use extended to poetry)—Desire for what is objectively perfect, inextricably the direction of historic and contemporary particulars.[7]

The poets he either included or named as meeting his criteria range from Pound, Eliot, Cummings, Stevens, and Moore to Bunting, McAlmon, Carnevali, Hemingway, and Whittaker Chambers. Among them, of course, are the three—George Oppen, Carl Rakosi, and Reznikoff—who together with Zukofsky were later to organize themselves into a cooperative publishing enterprise under the name Objectivist Press and who have become known (although they had not all even met one another until recently), as the "Objectivist" group proper. The statement of their Press principles showed how they spoke collectively when freed from the demands for a slogan; as drafted by Reznikoff, it read: "The Objectivist Press is an organization of poets who are printing their own work and that of others they think ought to be printed." So it is clear enough, that although Zukofsky (according to Rakosi) obtained the agreement of at least some of the others before using his label, he intended no strict program by it, and no manifesto was ever issued by the group.[8]

The bulk of Zukofsky's editorial space in that issue of *Poetry* is devoted to a long extract from an essay entitled "Sincerity and Objectification with Special Reference to the Work of Charles Reznikoff." In this we find both further explanation of Zukofsky's term, before he had thought of using it as a group name, and helpful insights into the special qualities of the contemporary he so much admired. "Objectification" refers primarily to structure: "the apprehension satisfied completely as to the appearance of the art form as an object." This looks very much like what Williams put more memorably a decade later, in the introduction to *The Wedge*:

To make two bald statements: There's nothing sentimental about a machine, and: A poem is a small (or large) machine made of words. When I say there's nothing sentimental about a poem I mean that there can be no part, as in any other machine, that is redundant.[9]

(Williams' *Collected Poems, 1934*, was the first publishing project of the Objectivist Press, although Williams himself was not personally engaged in the Press's activities.) That Reznikoff has remained true to this notion is clear from a text he has recently cited as expressing his convictions:

Poetry presents the thing in order to convey the feeling. It should be precise about the thing and reticent about the feeling.[10]

But Zukofsky himself, in his essay in *Poetry*, concludes that "The degree of objectification in the work of Charles Reznikoff is small." He gives one instance:

How shall we mourn you who are killed and wasted,
Sure that you would not die with your work unended—
As if the iron scythe in the grass stops for a flower.

and says of it, "Objectification in this poem is attained in the balance of the first two lines; the third line adds the grace of ornament in a simile, as might the design painted around a simple bowl." And he remarks, with what I take to be a touch of scorn, "The fact that it was originally an epitaph for Gaudier Brzeska may compel the attention of a few, but adds nothing to the poem as object." I confess, myself, to being compelled by the suppressed fact, which locates the poem in a specific time and place and reminds us inevitably of the Gaudier we have met through Pound's work. In any case, the revised text being well known, I have welcomed the chance to reprint the earlier version; it will be found below as poem 8, "On One Whom the Germans Shot."

But it is "sincerity" rather than "objectification" that Zukofsky chiefly praises Reznikoff for. He explains the term: "Writing occurs which is the detail, not mirage, of seeing, of thinking with the things as they exist, and of directing them along a line of melody." It is Reznikoff's "preoccupation with the accuracy of detail in writing—which is sincerity" that most earns Zukofsky's approval. He finds the quality both in the short poems and in the narrative verse, "perhaps the most neglected contribution to writing in America in the last ten years." And he continues, "the lives of Reznikoff's people slowly occur in the sincerity of the craft with which he has chosen to subdue them. One returns in the end...to the sincerity which has seen, considered, and weighed the tone these things have when rendered in only necessary words."

I take Zukofsky to be speaking of what is in effect the moral impressiveness of Reznikoff's poems—their weight in the reader's mind as of moral exempla. There is such a disinterested quieting of ego, such an openness to experience, such quickness of emotional response without either inflation or (usually) sentimentality, that one comes away from reading his work not merely charmed and revivified but—almost without one's having noticed it—edified. This is an old-fashioned kind of praise, and certainly edification is the last *intention* one could impute to the poems. But that freedom from intent is precisely the source or one of the sources of the impressiveness. *Ut doceat, ut moveat, ut delectet*—Pound has made the classical criteria current for moderns, and if his own occasionally strident didacticism has seemed the most obvious and undesirable mode for the "doceat," we should not let that prevent us from recognizing subtler kinds of moral value in writing.

The present book is intended to complement, not replace, the 1962 selection made by Reznikoff himself and published by New Directions as *By the Waters of Manhattan: Selected Verse*. It is justified on two counts: first, there is much good work, especially earlier poems, omitted from the 1962 book, and second, there is now a further decade's work to choose from. This has included not only the long work called *Testimony: The United States* in three volumes: 1885-1890 (New Directions, 1965), 1891-1900 (privately published, 1968) and 1901-1910 (not yet published). There is also the recently-completed unpublished book *Holocaust*, a work whose procedures are the same as those of *Testimony*—that is, verse paraphrase and quotation of selected portions of testimony from trial records. *Testimony* being, at least in part, available already, I have omitted selections from it to allow for more of *Holocaust*, whose grim and frightful subject-matter seems to demand that we subject ourselves to it more than briefly. In addition to these, the recent work includes a book of short poems as good as any Reznikoff has written, *By the Well of Living and Seeing and The Fifth Book of the Maccabees* (privately published, 1969), from which I print a generous selection, and the uncollected "Jews in Babylonia," which I print in full.

Each time Reznikoff has reprinted selections from his work—as he did in *Poems* (1920), drawing on the two earlier books; in *Five Groups of Verse* (1927), drawing on four earlier books; and in *By the Waters of Manhattan: Selected Verse* (1962)—he has freely rearranged the order of the poems. It is clear from this that the grouping of the poems, while a matter for thoughtful authorial decisions, remained flexible. Since it is impossible to reproduce the original groupings in a selection—and even in a complete collected edition one could only reproduce *one* of the available arrangements, of which there are as many as three for the earliest work —I have simply printed the poems in the relative order of the original sources. This does not mean, however, that one minor but real constituent element of the poems' effect on their first appearance has had to be sacrificed.

I have printed the texts as found in the source specified for each poem, without dropping the capitalization at the beginnings of lines as was done in the 1962 selection.

As for the choice of texts, my normal practice has, of course, been to print the latest one approved by the author. But with Mr. Reznikoff's generous permission, I have permitted myself a few exceptions, and I specify them here so that the author's toleration will not be interpreted as necessarily implying a reversal of his decisions of years ago. First, I restore to print three poems which the author dropped in later printings: numbers 3, 7, and 107. Second, I give earlier versions which I judge deserving of currency of two poems—numbers 8 and 10—the revisions of which are available in the 1962 selection. And third, I have allowed myself a taste of the freedom enjoyed by editors of an earlier age and printed eight poems—numbers 1, 6, 11, 12, 17, 18, 19, and 28—in versions earlier than those last revised by the author. My grounds for doing so are a combination of personal preference and historical interest. In all cases the Notes give details of the revisions later made so that the reader can judge my decisions for himself, and in the few instances where the revisions are extensive, the Notes print the later versions in full (numbers 11, 12, and 19). In these three cases I may claim the further justification that the early and later texts are so far apart as almost to constitute separate poems; while printing both I have given pride of place to the earlier ones to allow a clearer view of Reznikoff's development. In the cases of eighteen other poems I have followed more conventional editorial practice and printed the revised text in the body of the book, giving a full listing of variants in the Notes.

It will be seen then that one of the most valuable secondary uses of this selection is to allow a study of the poet's revisions, while not—I trust—interfering with those who simply want poems to read. As the interested reader compares, for instance, this poem of 1920 (number 19)—

Trees standing far off in winter
Against a polished blue sky
With boughs blown about like brown hair;

The stiff lines of the twigs
Blurred by the April buds;

Or branches crowded with leaves
And a wind turning
Their dark green light.

—with the stripped-down version of seven years later—

APRIL

The stiff lines of the twigs
Blurred by buds.

—he will appreciate even more the rhythmical economy and haiku-like condensation of the later version. Yet he may also share my reluctance to sacrifice the effect of the sequence of images in the first version, not to mention the lovely image in the last two lines, and he will be intrigued to notice that this version precedes by some three years the publication of Williams' "By the road to the contagious hospital" in *Spring and All* (1923). He will want both texts, then, and may agree with my choice to give priority to the 1920 text in its chronological place. Not that the possibility of "influence" on or by Williams is more than a distraction; the real point is the convergence of approach and treatment in the two poets (though the Williams poem, to be sure, encompasses more). Together, the three texts illustrate above all the potent presence of Pound—the Pound not only of the "Don'ts for Imagists" but also of *Cathay*.

Let me close by expressing my gratitude to my university for support in the form of a Summer Research Fellowship and above all to Charles Reznikoff, for his unfailing patient helpfulness and for the pleasure afforded both by his writing and by his serene and kindly presence.

Seamus Cooney
Western Michigan University
Kalamazoo

NOTES TO THE INTRODUCTION

[1]In conversation with the editor, June 1973.

[2]In *Contemporary Literature,* 10:2 (Spring 1969), 180. This issue is a special number on "The 'Objectivist' Poet" and contains interviews with Rakoski, Oppen, Zukofsky, and Reznikoff.

[3]Quoted from the version given in "A Retrospect," in *Literary Essays of Ezra Pound*, ed. T. S. Eliot (London, 1954), pp. 3-6.

[4]*Contemporary Poets*, ed. Rosalie Murphy (London, 1970), p. 914, where "without" is misprinted as "with."

[5]Introduction to Charles Reznikoff, *By the Waters of Manhattan: Selected Verse* (New York, 1962), p. xi.

[6]"By the well of living and seeing," Reznikoff explains, renders Luther's translation of what the Authorized Version gives as "from the way of the well Lahai-roi" (Genesis 24:62).

[7]*Poetry*, 37 (1930-1931), 268. All later quotations from Zukofsky are from this issue of *Poetry*.

[8]Rakosi in *Contemporary Literature*, 10:2 (Spring 1969), 179. For the Objectivist Press principles, see the same issue, p. 160.

[9]*Collected Later Poems of William Carlos Williams*, revised edition (New York, 1963), p. 4.

[10]*Contemporary Literature*, 10:2 (Spring 1969), 193.

By the Well of Living & Seeing

From

Rhythms

(1918)

[1]

In this room once belonging to me
The dead are walking silently.

I sank them six feet underground,
The dead are walking and no sound.

I raised on each a brown hill,
The dead are walking slow and still.

[2]

Her kindliness is like the sun
Toward dusk shining through a tree.

Her understanding is like the sun,
Shining through mist on a width of sea.

[3]

Look triumphantly
With your face's beauty
On others, not on me.
I see
In your green eyes two leaves
Of the forbidden tree.

[4]

The sea's white teeth
Nibble the cliff;
The cliff is a man,
Unafraid.

She eats his strength
Little by little,
His might will be lost
In her depths.

[5]

I step into the fishy pool
As if into a cool
Vault.
I, too, become
Cold-blooded, dumb.

[6]

They dug her grave so deep
No voice can creep
To her.

She can feel no stir
Of joy when her girl sings,
And quietly she sleeps
When her girl weeps.

[7]

Come away,
The clod in the mound
Will hear no sound
And the coffined stone
No moan.
Come away.

[8]

ON ONE WHOM THE GERMANS SHOT

How shall we mourn for you who are spilled and wasted,
Gaudier-Brzeska,
Sure that you would not die with your work unended,
As if the iron scythe in the grass stops for a flower?

From

Rhythms II

(1919)

[9]

I look across the housetops,
Through the leaves in a black pattern,
Where are you hidden, moon?

Surely I saw her,
Broad-bosomed and golden,
Coming toward us.

[10]

PESTILENCE

Streamers of crepe idling before doors.

Now the huge moon
At the end of the street like a house afire.

[11]

She moved effortless,
A swan on a still lake
Hardly beating the water with golden feet.

Straight brow and nose,
Curved lips and chin.

Sorrow before her
Was gone like noise from a street,
Snow falling.

[12]

I remember her all in white
In a house under great trees,
Shaded and still in summer;

A white curtain turning in her open window
And a swan dipping a white neck in the trees' shadow.

[13]

We heard no step in the hall.
She came
Sudden as a rainbow.

[14]

She who worked patiently,
Her children grown,
Lies in her grave patiently.

[15]

In the shop she, her mother, and grandmother,
Thinking at times of women at windows in still streets
Or women reading, a glow on resting hands.

From

Poems

(1920)

[16]

The sun was low over the blue morning water.
The waves of the bay were silent on the smooth beach
Where in the night the silver fish had died gasping.

[17]

Blocking hats with a boy helper
He tells of the sluts he visits.

Girls outshout the machines
And she strains for their words blushing.

Soon she too will speak
Their speech glibly.

[18]

The city breaks in houses to the sea, uneasy with waves,
And the lonely sun clashes like brass cymbals.
In the streets truck-horses, muscles sliding under the steaming
  hides,
Pound the sparks flying about their hoofs;
And fires, those gorgeous beasts, squirm in the furnaces
Under the looms weaving us.

At evening by cellars cold with air of rivers at night,
We, whose lives are only a few words,
Watch the young moon leaning over the baby at her breast
And the stars small to our littleness.

[19]

Trees standing far off in winter
Against a polished blue sky
With boughs blown about like brown hair;

The stiff lines of the twigs
Blurred by the April buds;

Or branches crowded with leaves
And a wind turning
Their dark green light.

[20]

Suddenly we noticed that we were in darkness.
So we went into the house and lit the lamp
And sat around, dark spaces about a sun.

The talk fell apart and bit by bit slid into a lake.
At last we rose and bidding each other good night went to our
    rooms.

In and about the house darkness lay, a black fog,
And each on his bed spoke to himself alone, making no sound.

[21]

In the streets children beneath tall houses at games greedily,
Remembering clocks, the house-cats lapping time.

[22]

She woke at a child crying
And turned to the empty cradle,
Forgetting.

[23]

Under the heavens furrowed with clouds
A man behind his stumbling plough.

From

Uriel Accosta:
A Play & A Fourth Group of Verse

(1921)

[24]

As he read, his mother sat down beside him. "Read me a little."
"You wouldn't understand, Ma." "What do you care? Read me
    a little.
When I was a girl I wanted to study so much, but who could?
My father used to cry when I talked to him about it,
But he cried because he couldn't afford to educate the boys—
    even."
As he read, she listened gravely; then went back to her ironing.
The gaslight shone on her round, ruddy face and the white cotton
    sheets that she spread and ironed;
From the shelf the alarm-clock ticked and ticked rapidly.

[25]

SUNDAY WALKS IN THE SUBURBS

On stones mossed with hot dust, no shade but the thin, useless
    shadows of roadside grasses;
Into the wood's gloom, staring back at the blue flowers on stalks
    thin as threads.

The green slime—a thicket of young trees standing in brown
    water;
With knobs like muscles, a naked tree stretches up,
Dead; and a dead duck, head sunk in the water as if diving.

The tide is out. Only a pool is left on the creek's stinking mud,
Someone has thrown a washboiler away.
On the bank a heap of cans;
Rats, covered with rust, creep in and out.
The white edges of the clouds like veining in a stone.

[26]

BEGGAR WOMAN

When I was four years old my mother led me to the park.
The spring sunshine was not too warm. The street was almost
    empty.
The witch in my fairy-book came walking along.
She stooped to fish some mouldy grapes out of the gutter.

[27]

Out of the hills the trees bulge;
The sky hangs in lumps of cloud.

[28]

VISITING (2)

He leans back along the sofa. I talk. His fingers twitch at his
    bath-robe.
Why am I taking trouble to please him? I talk. I turn my pockets
    inside out.
In his oblique eyes a polite disdain.

[29]

With broad bosom and hips, her head thrown back,
She parades, her high heels clacking,
Having conquered troublesome youth and not yet afraid of age.

[30]

On the counter were red slabs and rolls of beef. Bolognas hung
    along the walls and from the ceiling.
He carried his sliced bologna and two cents worth of bread to a
    table.
She came in and flung her muff upon the table, almost upon his
    bread.
Waiting to be served, she stood in front of the mirror,
Smoothing her dress over her hips, curving her arms to her hair,
    stretching herself.
She sat down facing him, smiled, and soon they were talking.
When she had gobbled her food, he gave her some of his.
He was through and still he sat there, warming himself at her
    quick beauty.
He had but to ask and he knew that she would come along.
He arose and went out. He walked down the street slowly, asking
    himself if he wasn't a fool.

[31]

PROVIDED FOR

Her father and mother were anxious to see her married and
    provided for as soon as possible.
Squat and ugly, her face pimpled, she was stupid and had just
    managed to get through grammar-school, two years older than
    her companions.
Her father wanted her to marry his clerk. He had a good-looking,
    womanish face.
She used to say, "He's marrying me for money, he hates me!"

Her father bought him a store in the Italian quarter.
The man who sold the store had it for years and had made money.
Her husband despised Italians. When they would not buy, he lost
    his patience, glared and shouted.
He sniffed at the men when they came in after a day's ditching,
    cheated when he could and still could not make the store pay.

His father-in-law bought him a store in another neighborhood. He
    could not make a living and was always borrowing.
Once his father-in-law refused him more money.
He came home. The two elder children were in bed. His wife was
    suckling the baby. She stared out of the window, tears in her
    eyes.
He slapped her face. "Tell your father! And if he doesn't help me
    out—!"

[32]

In a month they would be married.
He sang a song to himself in which her name was the only word.
His mother was waiting up for him. She said, "I was told to-day
    that her mother died an epileptic,

44

And her brother is an idiot in a home somewhere. Why didn't she
    tell you?''
He thought of hugging her narrow shoulders, comforting her;
Of noting their children's quirks and screeches fearfully—
How the moonlight had been glittering in her eyes.

[33]

A DESERTER

Their new landlord was a handsome man. On his rounds to collect
    rent she became friendly.
Finally, she asked him in to have a cup of tea. After that he came
    often.

Once his mouth jerked, and turning, she saw her husband in the
    doorway.
She thought, One of the neighbors must have told him.
She smiled and opened her mouth to speak, but could say nothing.
Her husband stood looking at the floor. He turned and went away.

She lay awake all night waiting for him.
In the morning she went to his store. It was closed.
She sent for his brothers and told them he had not been home.
    They went to the police. Hospitals and morgues were
    searched. For weeks they were called to identify drowned men.

His business had been prosperous; bank account and all were
    untouched. She and their baby girl were provided for.
In a few years they heard of him. He was dead.
He had been making a poor living in a far off city. One day he
    stepped in front of a street-car and was killed.

She married again. Her daughter married and had children. She
named none after her father.

[34]

At night, after the day's work, he wrote. Year after year he had
  written, but the right words were still not all there, the right
  rhythms not always used. He corrected the old and added new.
While away on a business trip he died. His children playing about
  the house, left home by the widow out at work, found the
  manuscript so carefully written and rewritten.
The paper was good to scribble on. Then they tore it into bits. At
  night the mother came home and swept it out.

[35]

He had a rich uncle who sent him to a university and would have
  taken him into the firm; but he went off and married a girl,
  the men of whose family were truckmen.
His uncle would have nothing to do with him, and he became a
  cigar peddler; but his wife was beautiful.
Even after she had borne children and had had to drudge and scrimp
  all her married life, whenever she came to his lodge ball, men
  and women turned to look at her.

His uncle died and left him a little money. And just in time,
  because he was growing too old to walk around at his business
  the way he had to.
He bought a formula for making an oil, rented a loft in which to
  manufacture, hired a salesman.
Perhaps the formula was a swindle, perhaps it was lack of
  experience in the business, but in a year or two he lost his
  money.

He went back to cigar peddling. His wife's hair had become white,
    but it gave her new beauty.

[36]

His father carved umbrella handles, but when umbrella handles
    were made by machinery, there was only one man for whom
    his father could work.
The pay was small, though it had once been a good trade.
They lived in the poorest part of the ghetto, near the lots where
    people dump ashes.
His father was anxious that his son should stay at school and get
    out of the mess he himself was in. "Learning is the best
    merchandise," he would say.
His father died; there was his mother to be taken care of. He
    taught in a school in the ghetto.
Some pupils came at nine and stayed until three; others came after
    public school and stayed until evening; most of the pupils
    came in the evening.
The courses were crammed, lasting a few months, pupils and
    teachers anxious to be rid of the matter as soon as possible.
So he worked day and night, week-days and Sunday.

His mother was dead. It was cold in the streets and windy. A dry
    snow had fallen and the feet of the walkers were turning it into
    brown sand.
He was forty.
Now he was free. To do what? He knew no one whom he cared to
    marry. And who would go into his poverty?
If he were to give up this work he knew so well, to what else could
    he turn?
He would just keep on. He had lost this world and knew there was
    no other.

He had a house of his own and a store. His wife took care of the
    store, and he at home studied Torah and Talmud.
His store was burned down. In those days they were not insured,
    but still he had the house.
He rented all of it but a room where he stayed and studied.
Once, when he was saying the morning prayer, Mendel, one of his
    tenants, came to him and said, "My son, the lawyer, has
    been arrested; won't you sign his bond here?"
It was not a bail bond but a deed; and in a few months Mendel
    made him move out of the house.
He went to a lawyer. The lawyer told him, "We can get the house
    back easily."
"What will they do to Mendel?" "Send him to Siberia." "Would
    it be right for me to put a Jew into the hands of *goyim?*"
He had to give children lessons on Hebrew. His son became a
    glazier. While working in another town his son died.
His daughter-in-law baked *begel* and his grandchildren sold them
    in the streets.

One day Mendel came to ask forgiveness.
He, too, had lost his money, and his son, too, the lawyer, had
    died.
He turned his face from Mendel; and so they stood, two old men.

When the club met in her home, embarrassed, she asked them not
    to begin: her father wanted to speak to them.
The members whispered to each other, "Who is her father?"
"I thank you, young men and women," he said, "for the honour
    of your visit. I suppose you would like to hear some
    of my poems." And he began to chant.

From

Five Groups of Verse

(1927)

[39]

I charge you, lips and teeth,
Keep watch upon my tongue:
Silence is legal tender everywhere.

[40]

DAWN

No one is on the lawn so early but the birds,
Sparrows and robbins pecking at the seeds
The wind has blown here; the wind itself is gone.

[41]

I have learnt the Hebrew blessing before eating bread;
Is there no blessing before reading Hebrew?

From

"Editing and Glosses"
in
By the Waters of Manhattan

(1929)

[42]

From KING DAVID

III: *Michal*

The grave men who will write
The history of the kings of Israel and of the wars of God,
Will not trouble to write of our happiness:
I had never hoped for a husband brave as Jonathan,
And handsomer than my father—
There is none like David among the young men.

What have I done that your father seeks my life?
God forbid! It is not so!
There is only a step between me and death:
As I sat before your father at meat—
In all that I have done have I not served him only?

Where is David?
He is sick.
Then we will bring him in his bed to the king.
Let us in!
    I cannot. He is sick.
Why have you fooled me and let my enemy escape?

From IV

You!
Paltiel,
You shall marry my daughter Michal,
Whom I have given to David,
For you are a good man, a quiet man.
And listen, all of you, and you, Jonathan,
Let me hear no more of this David—
Except to hear that he is dead.

From VI: *Ish-bosheth and Abner*

But I have come not to quarrel, but with a piece of news:
David sends me word that I should bring him Michal, whom Saul
    gave him as his wife.
Now send for her that I may bring her to David;
We must humor the king of Judah—
And your father was unjust to take her away and give her to
    another.
Look at Paltiel,
Whom Saul chose for a son-in-law;
Look at the tears in his eyes.
What, are you afraid to draw your sword at the Lion of Judah?
Well, well,

We shall let you run beside Michal,
Weeping all the way,
As we bring her to David.
But do not go a step beyond the border of Israel,
Or David's sword may take a swift dislike to you
At the thought of the five sons she has born you.

From VII

And yet the Michal that I knew
With all the airs that suited Saul's daughter
And pleased me, newly from the sheepfold.
The sweat and fingerprints of another man upon her.

From VIII

The Lord took me from following sheep
To be ruler of Israel,
And now He has given me rest from all my enemies.
Who am I, my God, and what is my house
That You have brought me so far?
I was surrounded
By the sorrows of death,
And the flood of ungodly men
Frightened me;
I cried to my God!
He shot out His lightnings;
He took me
And drew me out of the deep waters.
By Him
I have run through a troop,
And jumped over a wall;

He teaches my hands war,
To bend the bow;
He has given me my enemies:
I made them as dust before the wind;
I threw them away as dirt in the street.

IX: *David and Michal*

God—
Who chose me rather than your father and all his house
To be king of Israel;
But you shall die childless.

After you have hanged my sons,
From the eldest who was as tall as I
To the youngest who had not yet learned to walk:
This was my payment.
How much wiser was my father than his daughter or his son
    Jonathan!
What did you want now with me,
An aging woman who has had five children?
Only the tarnished glory that still is Saul's,
That you should have Saul's daughter for a wife.
Did you expect the girlish body,
The young and cheerful face I had?—
I knew you would not care for me,
That you had a hundred women, a thousand women,
And had sent for me,
Perhaps because the name of Saul was something still to you and
    your Jerusalem.
Now I see when they say
You found Saul in a cave asleep and caught your servant's hand
That would have killed him—

It was no kindness—
You knew Saul's time would come;
If you killed the Lord's Anointed,
There would have been war between you and Israel until your death.
And when you killed those who killed my brother Ish-bosheth,
You were the righteous man,
But you had all the profit of their wrong.
Joab you have not killed—who killed Abner—
Joab you need, you are afraid of Joab, he is your captain;
But Joab, too, will find you out some day, as I have found you out—
When his grey hairs go bloody to the grave.
    Your scribes will write you down a great king,
And of me—if they say anything at all—
But I belong to that doomed house of Saul
Not even Jonathan could save.
I shall not weep before you again;
These tears are the last:
Now I have wept them all away.
And I can speak of all my dead
Without a tear.
Your scribes will write me down a cold, proud woman,
Wandering about the garden of the king,
And you a glorious king, a glorious king.

From

Jerusalem the Golden

(1934)

[43]

In a strange street, among strangers,
I looked about: above the houses
you were there, sole companion many a night—
the moon.

[44]

On this beach the waves are never high:
broken on the sand bars, when they reach the shore—
a stranger might think the sea a bay
so gently do the waters splash and draw away.

The air is sweet, the hedge is in flower;
at such an hour, near such water, lawn, and wood,
the sage writing of our beginnings must have been:
lifting his eyes from the page he chanted,
''And God saw the earth and seas—that it was good.''

[45]

Going to work in the subway
this bright May morning
you have put on red slippers;
do they dance behind the counters
in the store, or about the machines
in the shop where you work?

[46]

The twigs of our neighbor's bush are so thin,
I can hardly see the black lines;
the green leaves seem to float in the air.

[47]

The bush with gaudy purple flowers is in the back yard—
seen only by its mistress, cats, and the white butterflies.

[48]

AUGUST

The trees have worn their leaves shabby.

[49]

RHETORIC

These streets, crowded an hour ago, are empty—
what crows that followed the armies of old

will be the scavengers?
The winds of night.

[50]

The branches about the street-lamp
are so thick with leaves, it shines
only on a flag of pavement;
leaf behind leaf the night rings.

[51]

SEPTEMBER

The blue luminous sky furrowed into clouds; the clear air
crowded with rain—the dark harvest.

[52]

AFTER RAIN

The motor-cars on the shining street move in semicircles of spray,
    semicircles of spray.

[53]

The morning light
is dim and blue—
the silent light
of woods; but now begins

the slight yet multitudinous
noise of rain.

[54]

Along the flat roofs beneath our window
in the morning sunshine,
I read the signature of last night's rain.

[55]

Rooted among roofs, their smoke among the clouds,
factory chimneys—our cedars of Lebanon.

[56]

LAMENT OF THE JEWISH WOMEN FOR TAMMUZ

Ezek. VIII. 14

Now the white roses, wilted and yellowing fast,
hang in the leaves and briers.

Now the maple trees squander their yellow leaves;
and the brown leaves of the oak have left Ur and become
    wanderers.

Now they are scattered over the pavements—
the delicate skeletons of the leaves.

60

[57]

I thought for a moment, The bush in the back yard has blossomed:
it was only some of the old leaves covered with snow.

[58]

A GARDEN

About the railway station as the taxicabs leave,
the smoke from their exhaust pipes is murky blue—
stinking flowers, budding, unfolding, over the ruts in the snow.

[59]

The days are long again, the skies are blue;
the hedges are green again, the trees are green;
only the twigs of the elms are dark.
At night the wind is cold again;
but by day the snow of your absence is melting:
soon May will be here and you the queen of the May.

[60]

It was in my heart to give her wine and dainties,
silken gowns, furs against the wind;
a woolen scarf,
coffee and bread was all that I could buy:
It is enough, she said.

It was in my heart to show her foreign lands,
at least the fields beyond the city:
I could not pay our way;

when she would see a row of street-lamps shining,
How beautiful, she would say.

[61]

If you ask me about the plans that I made last night
of steel and granite—
I think the sun must have melted them,
or this gentle wind blown them away.

[62]

The sun shining on the little waves of the bay, the little leaves
    of the hedge—
with these I school myself to be content.

[63]

LUZZATO
Padua 1727

The sentences we studied are rungs upon the ladder Jacob saw;
the law itself is nothing but the road;
I have become impatient of what the rabbis said,
and try to listen to what the angels say.
I have left Padua and am in Jerusalem at last, my friend;
for, as our God was never of wood or bone,
our land is not of stones or earth.

From JERUSALEM THE GOLDEN

(2) *The Shield of David*

Then spoke the prophets: Our God is not of clay,
to be carried in our saddle-bags;
not to be molten of silver or fine gold,
a calf to stand in our houses with unseeing eyes, unbending knees;
Who is the King of Glory?
He is from everlasting to everlasting;
we go down to the darkness of the grave,
but all the lights of heaven are His.

The smoke of your sacrifices is hateful, says the Lord,
I hate your festivals, your feasts, and your fasts;
worship Me in righteousness;
worship Me in kindness to the poor and weak,
in justice to the orphan, the widow, the stranger among you,
and in justice to him who takes his hire from your hand;
for I am the God of Justice, I am the God of Righteousness.

(4) *Karl Marx*

We shall arise while the stars are still shining,
while the street-lights burn brightly in the dawn,
to begin the work we delight in,
and no one shall tell us, Go,
you must go now
to the ship or office you work in
to waste your life for your living.
There shall be no more war, no more hatred;
none of us shall die of sickness;
there shall be bread and no one hunger for bread—

and fruit better than any a wild tree grew.
Wheels of steel and pistons of steel
shall fetch us water and hew us wood;
we shall call nothing mine—nothing for ourselves only.
Proclaim to the seed of man
throughout the length and breadth of the continents,
From each according to his strength,
to each according to his need.

From

In Memoriam: 1933

(1934)

[65]

POLAND: *ANNO* 1700

A N O L D J E W . There we were throughout Poland,
a Jew or two in each hamlet, a dozen in each village,
and a thousand or so in every town—
who knows how many thousands and tens of thousands—
going about in the dust of summer
or against the cold wind with noses deep in our collars,
hands pushed into our sleeves,
selling and buying—
this lord's cow and that lord's sack of wheat,
scheming as hard to earn our bread
as a minister might to rule a kingdom,
when, crash!
as a dish slips from a woman's hands
and lies in pieces on the ground,
our bustling ended,

and we were scurrying from the Cossacks
straight for the towns—
their bands trotting along the roads,
booty hanging about their saddles,
lances tall as the chimneys;
many a Jew and Pole were skewered together
on those lances, or hanged
side by side with a pig between them—
boughs were heavy with that harvest;
and still the Cossacks came
breeding in the plunder,
until cannon no longer stopped them,
and gates of towns could not keep them out—
Kiev was taken;
the dead along highway and byway,
pools of blood in streets and houses
drew the troops of them on their swift horses out of the steppes,
many and pitiless as insects.

A YOUNG JEW. How tiresome these old stories are—
Assyrians and Syrians,
now Germans and now the Cossacks;
how the Cossacks plundered and killed the Jews of Poland
or that the glory of the Jews in Spain
was muddied
as sunshine on a pool by cattle.
Tell us of the Jews along the Rhine
before the crusades; before the Inquisition,
upon the plains from which the snowy Pyrenees are seen;
tell us of our glory in Babylon,
of our glory in Egypt,
that we who in the alleys and the byways
of these Polish cities
have only synagogues of wood,

who in the fairs and marketplaces sweat or freeze beside our
    booths and wagons
from dawn to darkness,
may hide that splendor
in our hearts.

THE OLD JEW. As soldiers in their drill
charge and beat back the charge
of a foe they may never meet,
so we strengthen ourselves
in struggling with our father's foes, long harmless
and merely the people of our thoughts—
but some day ready again to act in flesh and blood,
surely as a hard winter brings the wolves howling
along the forest roads and even to the streets.

ANOTHER JEW. These are the pools
where the marketplace is sunken,
but the ground is wet
and the rain is falling everywhere.
The wind is blowing in every street—
only banging a shutter
or whirling up dust
in a corner;
but it will blow a storm again.
Unravel this world
with your nervous fingers
and reweave the knotted thread
on the loom of the Talmud;
sort the dirty rags of the world,
buyers of old clothes, ragpickers;
gather the bits
and refine it in the fire of the Torah,
dealers in junk;

peddlers and keepers of stands and booths,
and even you who have stores on the streets,
you great merchants who buy flax in Russia
and ship furs to Germany,
I have heard it said there is no goods like the Talmud,
no goods like the Torah.
The sun was heavy on my head,
the earth was hot beneath my shoes
in the alley
that led to other alleys
and other alleys,
but I stepped into the garden,
into the cool palace of the Torah.

A YOUNG JEW. You look at the world through printed pages—
dirty panes of glass;
and even if the pages are the Talmud
and those who have written wrote with diamonds,
the more they scratched, less clearly we can see.
I see neither rag nor bark,
flesh nor leaf,
I feel neither sticks nor stones,
cloth nor pillow,
neither rain nor snow nor wind nor sunshine;
I see God only and my spirit brightens
like a mirror;
I touch Him touching all I touch;
on earth I am as close to Him as those in Heaven.
Could I teach myself to want nothing,
nothing could be taken from me;
I should be unafraid of today or tomorrow,
and live in eternity like God.
Cold and hunger, pain and grief
do not last,

are mortal like myself;
only the joy in God has no end—
this it is that in the wind
showers the petals upon the grass,
whirls up the glistening snow,
or sweeps the dust along the streets before the storm;
it shines into me
as the sun upon a tree in winter
after rain.
Light becomes colors,
colors
light and shadows—
dusk and dawn;
tasting God in the salt water
and the sweet rain,
I sink and my feet have nothing to rest on,
I rise and my hands find nothing to hold,
and am carried slowly,
now swiftly,
towards night and towards noon.

From

Separate Way

(1936)

[66]

EPITAPHS

I

Drowning
I felt for a moment reaching towards me
finger tips against mine.

II

You mice,
that ate the crumbs of my freedom,
lo!

III

The clock strikes:
these are the steps of our departure.

A brown oak leaf
scraping the sidewalk
frightened me.

Proserpine
swallowed only six seeds
of the pomergranate
and had to stay six months among the dead—
I was a glutton.

[67]

WALKING AND WATCHING

I

Summer Evening

The black sloop at anchor
has a light in the rigging;
the waters of the river
twinkle;
the stars spring up
on the smooth twilight;

row after row,
the street lamps burst into light.

with stone hatchets, or with a shell too dull
to cut the sinews;
and in the stumps of our thumbs drove up spikes
until the elbow;
but so great the help of Jesus,
with this maimed hand I, Isaac Jogues,
Jesuit and priest,
baptised an Indian among the captives,
using the raindrops on a long leaf of corn.)

Let others cry, "New lands!
where Indians shall bring
kernels of gold, wagons full of gold;
whatever spills upon the way
we shall tread carelessly,
for we shall have so much of gold—
so many pearls to sew upon our clothes;
away,
unthrifty gentlemen,
to the forests of Virginia!
There are lands
to feed all the poor of England,
trees
to build each a home;
give us but axes, shovels, and ploughshares,
and away then to America,
all you poor!"
In England a watch is set about us
and we are clapt in jails,
and Holland is a dear place,
for there they live by trading—
but we are a plain country people
whose trade is husbandry,
and we would worship God as simply as the shepherds

II

The branches,
sloping towards each other,
sway in the wind;
the leaves quiver
in the rain;
flashing when the lightning flashes,
drops of rain
become falling sparks.

III

Desert

The swift river, foaming into waves,
waves bursting into foam,
mile after mile,
under a windless and unclouded sky;
not a beast or bird,
neither tree nor bush, no weed or grass:
a plain of white sand
on which are scattered
black stones and boulders,
or ledge on ledge
rising in barren cliffs.

IV

The water is freezing in straight lines across the ripples;
the ice is so thin the brown leaves
are seen moving along underneath;
the wheels of the automobiles hiss
on the wet pavement;

the bridge has become only a few lines in pencil
on the grey sky—
even lines made by ruler and compass.

The street curves in and out, up and down
in great waves of asphalt;
at night the granite tomb is noisy with starlings
like the creaking of many axels;
only the tired walker knows how much there is to climb,
how the sidewalk curves into the cold wind.

[68]

NEW NATION*

I

Land of Refuge

A mountain of white ice
standing still
in the water
here forty fathoms deep
and flowing swiftly
from the north;
grampuses and whales
going by in companies,
spouting up water in streams
(these wonders of the Lord, I, Francis Higginson,
saw on the way to Salem);
a fair morning,

---

*I am indebted to Albert Bushnell Hart's *American History Told by Contemporaries* for much that I have used. C.R.

74

and still many leagues from land,
but the air warm and spiced—
yellow flowers on the sea,
sometimes singly,
sometimes in sheets;
high trees on every hill and in every dale,
on every island,
and even on the stony cliffs;
banks of earth
on which are groves of trees,
and no undergrowth of bush or brambles;
the sandy shore overrun with vines
of melons and of grapes
which the beat and surging of the sea
overflows
(this I, Arthur Barlowe, saw);
trees of sweet-smelling wood
with rind and leaves sweet-smelling
as the bark of cinnamon and leaves of bay;
soil dark and soft,
strawberries everywhere,
hickory nuts and sassafras;
here are grapes white and red,
very sweet and strong,
and plums, black and red,
and single roses, white and red and damask;
we have eaten venison with the Indians,
and drunk water with spice in it—
Indian corn, even the coarsest,
makes as pleasant a meat as rice.
(Without any show of anger
the Iroquois crunched our fingers in their mouths,
and with their teeth tore off the nails;
then hacked our fingers off, joint by joint,

75

and Galilean fishermen,
live as plainly;
away,
dissenters,
to New England!
A great wind blowing,
heavy rain—
thick darkness;
the sailors running here and there,
shouting at one another
to pull at this and at that rope,
and the waves pouring over the ship;
landing in the rain—
the cold rain
falling steadily;
the ground wet,
all the leaves dripping
and the rocks running with water;
the sky is cloud on cloud
in which the brief sun barely shines,
the ground snow on snow,
the cold air
wind and blast;
we have followed our God
into this wilderness
of trees heavy with snow,
rocks seamed with ice,
that in the freezing blasts
the remnant of this remnant
kindle so bright, so lasting a fire
on this continent,
prisoners of ice and darkness everywhere
will turn and come to it
to warm their hands and hearts.

II

Brief History

Glaciers pushing so far and surely
thaw and withdraw;
even the deep,
while the explosion of its waves
dynamites the cliffs,
leaves new lands,
new groves and habitations
beside the glittering currents flowing quickly
into the silver waters of the sun.

Here are men who find
a comfortable bed
among the rocks,
who wrap themselves
in their coats
to sleep upon the ground
while their horse feeds in the grass beside the lake;
who catch trout in the brook
and roast them on the ashes;
eat the flesh
of bear for meat, the white meat of turkeys
for their bread, and whose salt is brought
in an iron pot across the mountains;
who live
where two hundred acres may be had
for a calf and a wool hat;
or walk where there is no road
nor any man, except the savage.

All the bells of Boston

are tolling
a solemn peal;
the market men will take no more paper money—
hard money only:
soldiers with bare feet showing through their shoes
in the snow, the smoke of the camp-fires blowing into their eyes;
for food a bowl of beef soup full of burnt leaves;
no house or hut, and even the sick in tents.
The rays of your light,
like the sun's, Republic of France,
shone first in the west; the eater shall give meat,
and out of the strong sweetness—
out of the bones of the French monarchy
the honey of freedom;
the bells of Philadelphia are ringing
as if for a fire,
and the crowds,
shouting and hallooing,
fill the streets;
ring, bells, throughout the night,
let no one sleep;
ring, clash, and peal
until the log cabins and cottages of cedar shingles,
the houses of grey stone or of brick,
tremble,
and the listeners
feel in their flesh
the vibrations of your metal voices
ringing,
Proclaim liberty,
proclaim liberty throughout the land!

Wrongs,
like molecules of gas that seep into a house,

explode
in particles of fire!
A captain gallops down the street,
wheels,
and the hoof of his horse
sends the pie plates shining in the sun;
his horse stops
at what is
flowing from the battlefield,
sniffs at it, and will not cross:
this is not water—
it is blood
in a thick and ropy stream.
(The dying negress says,
I cannot eat dry hominy:
I lived in *massa's* house,
and used to have white bread and coffee;
and I want something sweet in my mouth.)
On the lawn the negroes dance
and clap their hands,
So glad! so glad!
Bless the Lord for freedom!
So glad! so glad!

Do not mourn the dandelions—
that their golden heads become grey
in no time at all
and are blown about in the wind;
each season shall bring them again to the lawns;
but how long the seeds of justice
stay underground,
how much blood and ashes of precious things
to manure so rare and brief a growth.

Currents of waste
wind
along the river
between the factories—
the colonnades
and sacred groves
of chimneys;
where once the road
in ruts and ridges—lines of rails
hold to a gleaming purpose,
come wind, come rain, come winter or the night;
build storey on storey out of glass;
light electric lights,
row after row, whose shining wires
will not flicker in the wind;
let the streets sound
with the horns and hosannahs of motor cars!
Man, you need no longer
drudge at plow or oar, no longer trudge;
proclaim this liberty to all!
If bread may be as plentiful,
shall we not share it
as we share water?

From

Going To and Fro and Walking Up and Down

(1941)

[69]

From A SHORT HISTORY OF ISRAEL; NOTES AND GLOSSES

I

The prince who once left an ancient city
for the sands in which were only snakes and lizards,
the vulture and the owl—wilderness that led to wilderness—
has become this stranger,
whose pillow is a stone,
who leads a flock from well to well
no faster than the lambs can walk,
afraid
of those whose water and whose land it is;

the servant who once served a master well—
Potiphar and Pharaoh—has become a tribesman with matted hair,
this slave, the son of a slave;
a desert fox

83

become a faithless dog, fawning
upon the sleek Egyptian for a fish,
afraid,
and snarling at the whip
that lifts him from his sleep.

The water is bitter—you must learn to drink it;
the food you gather will not last—
wormy by morning;
you must gather it again.

Your enemies have forbidden you this peace—
this place;
you will find another—
a land of milk and honey,
of springs and fruit trees.

The timid folk that once ran before the horses of their masters
into the wilderness
to cry out at last for bread and remember with longing
the fish and cool melons of Egypt and find nothing
except pools of bitter water to drink—
serpents underfoot and swords in the hands of enemies,
until the weak and meek, the kind and gentle, died,
have become these savages
from the rocks

who troop down howling
to take no man alive
either to draw water or gather twigs,
to whom the women and their children are as baleful,
who burn pots and jugs,
clothing and ornaments,
in the fire

that leaves a heap of blackened stones
where once a quiet people lived;
those wanderers who, fainting in the
heat of day and freezing by night,
still led a few sheep and goats
from wilderness to wilderness, picking their food
from the bushes and scrabbling in the sand for roots,
are now these churls,
become fat
in fenced cities and walled towns—
in ivory houses,

among olive trees and fig trees, vineyards
and fields of barley and wheat,
with cattle feeding beside streams and fattening in stalls,
with men servants and maid servants,
jugs of oil and jars of wine, jewels of silver and jewels of gold;
for whom the Tyrians
bring embroidered shirts and swords with jewelled hilts
and slaves with sticks
to run before the chariot shouting, "Kneel, kneel!"

This meat is forbidden—you must not eat it;
lusts of the belly and the loins!
Your neighbor's house, your neighbor's cattle,
your neighbor's wife, and the stranger's god—
all are forbidden!

Be just
to each other, to your servant, to the needy and stranger;
for you were needy in the wilderness
and servants and strangers in Egypt.

Those who were farmers and herdsmen

in the villages of Judah
owners of vineyards and olive-yards in the hills—
far from great rivers and cities,
walking slowly as their cattle,
and for whom time was measured slowly
by the seasons,
now live from day to day among the weeds
where the streets end

and the sewers of Babylon empty
into the river,
hurry along,
searching the gutter and rubbish heaps
or selling salt
in the bustle of Rome—
are now carried by the waves and winds
to the uttermost islands and lands,
exiles and captives;

those who left their land
for all the neighboring countries—
standing in the puddles of the galleys
or following
the chariots, chained together,
to be howled at in towns
and stared at
by the shepherds—

are these Jews
in the cities of Persia and Spain,
in Egypt and England,
who have houses of stone and green fields,
chests heavy with coins and books,
who ride out gingerly on mules and horses

to sell damask and furs and spice,
lend money to the lords,
and become uneasy physicians and counsellors of kings.

Among men who gorge and swill
and sleep in their vomit,
be temperate and clean;
among men who lust and whore
be true; among men in armor
be men of peace; among men in robes who fast and scourge
*   themselves and go about*
in hair shirts, preaching love and hell fire,
be men of sense; among men who torture
be Jews.

Those who lived in villages and alleys,
in huts and cellars,
selling a calf shrewdly
and buying a sack of wheat cheap
to sell cupfuls
for a copper—
who were pillaged and murdered
in the cities of Germany,
in Spain and Russia,

from York to Ispahan—
their sons
stand up to plead—
in every language—
for the poor
and wronged,
teach by formula and picture,
speech and music—
heal and save!

You who envied Edom
and were afraid of
Egypt, whose soldiers were like the sands for number,
like the stars,
Judah was buried in Jerusalem
to flourish;
burnt—
to step out of the sea
among breaking waves.

IV

Wouldn't they have been surprised, Saint Louis and his knights,
still bleeding from the scimitars,
if, crowding forward to greet the Queen of Heaven,
she were to turn from them and say, pointing to a wretched Jew,
"The bravest of you all is he,
who alone,
hedged in by monks and knights, by staves and swords,
in answer to your question
still denied me!"

From *Autobiography: New York*

[70]

I am alone—
and glad to be alone;
I do not like people who walk about
so late; who walk slowly after midnight
through the leaves fallen on the sidewalks.
I do not like
my own face

in the little mirrors of the slot-machines
before the closed stores.

[71]

Walking along the highway,
I smell the yellow flowers of a shrub,
watch the starlings on a lawn, perhaps—
but why are all these
speeding away in automobiles,
where are they off to
in such a hurry?
They must be going to hear wise men
and to look at beautiful women,
and I am just a fool
to be loitering here alone.

[72]

I like the sound of the street—
but I, apart and alone,
beside an open window
and behind a closed door.

[73]

Bright upon the table
for your birthday,
the burning candles will dissolve
in rays
and lumps of wax.

Unlike a skull,
they say politely,
This is you!

[74]

I am afraid
because of the foolishness
I have spoken.
I must diet
on silence;
strengthen myself
with quiet.

Where is the wisdom
with which I may be medicined?
I will walk by myself
and cure myself
in the sunshine and the wind.

[75]

THE BRIDGE

In a cloud bones of steel.

[76]

GOD AND MESSENGER

This pavement barren

as the mountain
on which God spoke to Moses—
suddenly in the street
shining against my legs
the bumper of a motor car.

[77]

A beggar stretches out his hand
to touch a fur collar, and strokes it unseen,
stealing its warmth for his finger tips.

[78]

Stream that a month ago
flowed between banks of snow
and whose grey ripples showed
a sky as grey—
now the stream is seen
clear and as green
as are the willows on its banks,
for it is May:
this stream was turbid, grey,
that now is clear and green—
for it is May!

Your hair be dyed and curled the more,
your dress be gayer than before—
your beauty had its praise,
your anxious eyes now ask it;
but your face will soon be crumpled
like a ball of paper tossed

in the trash-basket,
in the trash-basket.

From *Autobiography: Hollywood*

[79]

I wish that they were with me here
to walk under the palms
and feel the silken air—
my wife, three thousand miles away, my mother,
farther yet, being dead.

You write that you work and are tired.
I know—and remember your dream:
I was looking at the stars and saying
they were like this and like that,
and you, my wife, beside me,
making similes better than mine—
when an animal ran out of the bushes
to bite your foot and gnaw it; you screamed and I,
horrified and compassionate,
stood bravely watching.

[80]

RAINY SEASON

It has been raining for three days.
The faces of the giants
on the bill-boards
still smile,

but the gilt has been washed from the sky:
we see the iron world.

The gutters are gurgling and the water is over the curbs,
lapping the pavement, even the walls; the gulls are flying—
flying to the dark mountains before another storm.
The cormorants are leaving
the ridges of the sea—
the cold wind and black fog and the noise of the sea.

[81]

An actress
powdered yellow for the camera—
daughter of the Greek princess buried in Mycenae
with a gold mask on her face. The hush
when into the restaurant crowded with faces
a star comes:
the painted lips are silent, the painted eyes turn.
The Mexican has finished playing;
he lifts his guitar and kisses it.

[82]

These gentlemen are great; they are paid
a dollar a minute. They will not answer
if you say, Good morning;
will neither smile nor nod—
if you are paid only a dollar or two
an hour. (Study
when to be silent, when to smile.)
The director who greets my employer loudly

and smiles broadly, reaching for his hand and back,
scowls and glares at my greeting. Now I understand
why he managed to give me only his fingers
when we were introduced. Why do you go to such trouble
to teach me that you are great?
I never doubted it until now.

[83]

At twilight, twenty years or so ago,
two or three mice would come into the room,
in and out
under the radiator beside the desk;
now
two or three sparrows stop at the window
to chirp a while—pleasanter company.
Surely, I am not unblessed of God.

[84]

I will not question the sunshine
that shines so pleasantly
on my face. I know the answer:
it will not last—for me.

Tomorrow it will rain, we say, and tomorrow is as clear as
        yesterday;
the mountains are green and yellow—clear of mist;
and the sea, free of fog, is bluer than ever.
But we do not believe this sunshine;
it will not last, we say darkly:
an earthquake will tumble a wall upon our heads
or a thorn scratch a finger and we shall die.

[85]

The cloudy afternoon is as pleasant
as silence. Who would think
one would ever have enough of sunshine?
A good epitaph, I suppose, would be
He liked the sunshine;
better still, *He liked to walk.*
And yet the dead, if it could speak, might say,
I had grown tired of walking,
yes, even of the sunshine.

[86]

I will take off my coat and tie; unbutton
my collar; sit in a soft chair;
cross my legs and close my eyes;
open them only
to see the bush in front of the window
stir in the wind.
The bush in front of the window is crowded
with bunches of red flowers among the narrow leaves:
flowers and leaves
have the same colorless shadow.

The single fly that went jerkily about is
resting somewhere;
outside a bird is chirping slowly
a single note.
The room is growing dark,
but the brass knob of the closed door shines—
ready for use.

HEROICS

In the discipline I set myself
a spoonful of porridge is a breach;
how much more a careless word.
I charge you, Captain Abstinence, put down the rebels;
and you, Captain Diligence, see to the borders—
where are the laurels
to hide my grey hair?

To march, to hurry, yes, to hide day after day,
month after month, eating, so they say, bread green with mould
and drinking water green with scum
to live, crowded in camps or in ditches or alone in a pit,
but glad to be alive, losing day after day,
year after year, perhaps life itself,
at the beck of others;
yet you boggle
at a little hunger, a little thirst.

The forty winks you oversleep, the blade of grass you overeat—
this is the straw that will break your back at last.
If you were walking along a highway,
a step to the right or left
would not matter at all;
but, if you must climb the rocks of the wild goats,
watch yourself.

I never tasted food that was better
than the bread and apples I used to buy
for a dime; nor anything to drink
better than water from the faucet
after a long walk.
Here beggar, three pennies—

your fare to serenity:
abstinence, reticence, diligence—
hunger, silence, and sweat.

[88]

From TESTIMONY

IV

Outside the night was cold, the snow was deep
on sill and sidewalk; but in our kitchen
it was bright and warm.
I smelt the damp clothes
as my mother lifted them from the basket,
the pungent smell of melting wax
as she rubbed it on the iron,
and the good lasting smell of meat and potatoes
in the black pot that simmered on the stove.
The stove was so hot it was turning red.
My mother lifted the lid of the pot
to stir the roast with a long wooden spoon:
Father would not be home for another hour.
I tugged at her skirts. Tell me a story!

Once upon a time (the best beginning!)
there was a rich woman, a baroness, and a poor woman, a beggar.
The poor woman came every day to beg and every day
the rich woman gave her a loaf of bread
until the rich woman was tired of it.
I will put poison in the next loaf, she thought,
to be rid of her.
The beggar woman thanked the baroness for that loaf

97

and went to her hut,
but, as she was going through the fields,
she met the rich woman's son coming out of the forest.
"Hello, hello, beggar woman!" said the young baron,
"I have been away for three days hunting
and am very hungry.
I know you are coming from my mother's
and that she has given you a loaf of bread;
let me have it—she will give you another."
"Gladly, gladly," said the beggar woman,
and, without knowing it was poisoned, gave him the loaf.
But, as he went on, he thought, I am nearly home—
I will wait.
You may be sure that his mother was glad to see him,
and she told the maids to bring a cup of wine
and make his supper—quickly, quickly!
"I met the beggar woman," he said,
"and was so hungry I asked for the loaf you gave her."
"Did you eat it, my son?" the baroness whispered.
"No, I knew you had something better for me
than this dry bread."
She threw it right into the fire,
and every day, after that, gave the beggar woman a loaf
and never again tried to poison her.
So, my son, if you try to harm others,
you may only harm yourself.

And, Mother, if you are a beggar, sooner or later,
there is poison in your bread.

From

Inscriptions: 1944-1956

(1959)

[89]

It was raining and the street
empty. I passed an old woman selling newspapers.
As I bought one
I glanced at her feet.
"So big
in these rubbers.
But it's better than to get them wet," she added,
dubious, "and be sick.
A man lent them. They are rubbers for a man, not me,
and I have to tie them on with a string.
But how big my feet look!" I looked at her again:
only this was left—vanity.

From
MEDITATIONS ON THE FALL AND WINTER HOLIDAYS

Feast of Booths

This was a season of our fathers' joy:
not only when they gathered grapes and the fruit of trees
in Israel,
but when, locked in the dark and stony streets,
they held—symbols of a life from which they were banished
but to which they would surely return—
the branches of palm trees and of willows, the twigs of the myrtle,
and the bright odorous citrons.

This was the grove of palms with its deep well
in the stony ghetto in the blaze of noon;
this the living stream lined with willows;
and this the thick-leaved myrtles and trees heavy with fruit
in the barren ghetto—a garden
where the unjustly hated were justly safe at last.

In booths this week of holiday
as those who gathered grapes in Israel lived
and also to remember we were cared for
in the wilderness—
I remember how frail my present dwelling is
even if of stones and steel.

I know this is the season of our joy:
we have completed the readings of the Law
and we begin again;
but I remember how slowly I have learnt, how little,
how fast the year went by, the years—how few.

[91]

Again cool windy days,
grey skies and sidewalks black with rain;
again the solitary walks,
and a quiet room in which to sit and work
and see mankind—
only through a windowpane.

[92]

Now on our way through the park one meets
birds not unlike the sparrows of our streets
but smaller and colored a softer grey—
without the sparrow's brownish hue
and with a tinge of green, a hint of white:
a soothsayer might read a message in their flight
and I can spell a good omen, too.

[93]

From NOTES ON THE JEWISH HOLIDAYS

Hanukkah

In a world where each man must be of use
and each thing useful, the rebellious Jews
light not one light but eight—
not to see by but to look at.

[94]

NIGHT-PIECE

I was within the shadows of the yard the shed
and saw the snow upon its roof—
an oblong glowing in the moonlit night.

I could not rest or close my eyes,
although I knew that I must rise
early next morning and begin my work again,
and begin my work again.

That day was lost—that month as well;
and year and year for all that I can tell.

[95]

EXODUS*

We who had known the desert's grit and granite,
saw the river, the wide and brimming river,
watering the fields of wheat and barley,
of cucumbers and onions, and bringing fish for food.
Come, he had said, I am no Egyptian—
who fears and hates the tribesmen of the desert—
I am your brother, Joseph.
Come and bring your herds and flocks;
here is land, ample land, for grazing;
here is plenty; come and prosper.

We who had known the desert's angry god,
saw the well-ordered life of Egypt,

*The three lines at the very end of the third stanza and those at the
end of the last stanza (lines 13-15) are from the Mishnah (Hullin 3:3
and other places, Danby's translation). C.R.

its fields and ancient cities;
shelter from the heat by day, the wind at night;
saw the ancient river, wide and brimming—
all of Egypt's plenty;
and, turning to each other who had famished in the desert,
languished in the desert,
said: let us stay in Egypt;
here the gods are many—kind and wise.

But there came a Pharaoh who knew not Joseph
and set us building treasuries and cities,
set us making brick for him and building cities:
we who had been masters of our days and daylight,
free to wander, free to stay.
King and servants, priests and laymen;
soldiers, overseers, and slaves:
this was Egypt's peace and order,
and in this order we were slaves:
Israel like a bird that a creeping weasel has wounded in the head
or a man knocked against a wall;
the cattle have trampled it—but still it flutters.

But there came a shepherd from the desert,
speaking in the ancient tongue
all but our eldest had forgotten;
and we saw an old man—withered hands and haunches;
and he said to us, stuttering as he spoke:
I bring a message from the God of your fathers
and, in place of these burdens,
I bring you—the yoke of His law.
How pleasant it is, distinguished from the beasts,
to feed upon His law,
tasting in each syllable
the radiance of our Lord!

If there is bone enough to make the tooth of a key
and ink enough to write two letters of the alphabet—
then fear not the rush of tramping shoes nor the sound of the
*   shouting*
and hurry out of this land!

From

By the Well of Living and Seeing
and
The Fifth Book of the Maccabees

(1969)

"And Isaac came from the way
of the well Lahai-roi...."
Genesis 24:62

[96]

My grandfather, dead long before I was born,
died among strangers; and all the verse he wrote
was lost—
except for what
still speaks through me
as mine.

[97]

My grandmother in her old age
sold barley and groats at a stall
in the marketplace. She did not measure her cereal
more carefully
than I must minutes.

[98]

The dying gull
alone on a rock,
wings spread and unable to fly,
lifting its head—
now and then—
with a sharp cry.

[99]

Horsefly,
on the window of the automobile agency:
you're out of business now.

[100]

Ah, the drill
breaking open the pavement
again—
and yet again.
This is the nightingale
that sings in our streets.

[101]

This Puerto Rican—just an ordinary laborer—
how he goes to his work in the park
jauntily
swinging his rake
like a cane!

[102]

The pigeon saunters along the path—
towards me.
Will it turn aside?
Of course.
Not only Athena's owl
knows the history of man.

[103]

A grove of small trees, branches thick with berries,
and within it the constant twitter of birds.
The trees of the park this cold windy day
for want of leaves
are hung with paper—strips of dirty paper.

[104]

The autumn rains have begun
but are over for the moment;
leaves float
on the pools of water on the pavement.
The lonely walker hears
only the swift motor-cars.

[105]

MILLINERY DISTRICT

Many fair hours have been buried here
to spring up again as flowers—
on hats.

[106]

LA BELLE DAME SANS MERCI

White, bloodless face, red eyes
and tight bitter mouth.

[107]

LESSON IN ARCHAEOLOGY

The writing on clay
baked in the fire of the palace
has outlasted
the writing baked in the sun.

[108]

SIMILES

Indifferent as a statue
to the slogan
scribbled on its pedestal.

The way an express train
snubs the passengers at a local station.

Like a notebook forgotten on the seat in the 'bus,
full of names, addresses and telephone numbers:
important, no doubt, to the owner—
and of no interest whatever
to anyone else.

Words like drops of water on a stove—
a hiss and gone.

[109]

THE OLD MAN

The fish has too many bones
and the watermelon too many seeds.

[110]

The man who planned the bridge
had his foot crushed between the piling and the dock
by a ferryboat. That was useless, ferryboat!
He died
but the ferryboats, too, are gone.

[111]

EPITAPH

Not the five feet of water to your chin
but the inch above the tip of your nose.

[112]

EPILOGUE

Blessed
in the light of the sun and at the sight of the world
daily,
and in all the delights of the senses and the mind;
in my eyesight, blurred as it is,
and my knowledge, slight though it is,
and my life, brief though it was.

Leaving the beach on a Sunday in a streetcar
a family of three—mother, son and daughter:
the mother, well on in the thirties, blond hair, worried face;
the son, twelve years of age or so, seated opposite,
and the daughter, about eight or nine, beside her.
The boy was blond, too; a good-looking little fellow
with dreamy eyes. The little girl was quite plain;
mouth pulled down at the corners,
sharp angry eyes behind eyeglasses.

No sooner were they seated than the boy, speaking gently, said,
"Today was one of the most wonderful days I ever had."
The girl said shrilly, "I wish we could live in one of those
        houses"—
looking at the bungalows along the shore—
"then we could go to the beach every day."
The mother did not answer either.
The beach they were coming from was crowded with poor people;
and the family was dressed cheaply but was neat and spotless,
even after the day's outing.
I wondered idly where the father was: at work? dead? divorced?

After a while the mother said, weighing her words,
"You know Mister..."
I did not hear the name: it was spoken so softly.
She was talking to the boy.
"He goes fishing every Wednesday.
I think I can get him to take you along."
The boy did not answer for a minute or two
and then said, in his gentle voice,
"I should like it very much."
"Can I go too?" asked the little girl shrilly,
but no one answered her.

Mother and son had eyes only for each other.
She took out her handkerchief and wiped his face.
He complained of something in his eye—
certainly not enough to make him blink—
and she raised the upper lid
and lowered the lower lid to look for it.
The little girl stood up to look out of the window
and the boy said to his mother, ''She stepped on my toes
and did not even say, Excuse me, please.''
The mother turned to the little girl and said sharply,
''Why didn't you say, Excuse me?
You should have said, Excuse me, brother.''
The little girl said nothing,
face turned toward the window,
the corners of her mouth far down and her eyes,
bright and dry, looking sharply through her glasses.

[114]

Would I write a letter for him?
Insignificant-looking, rather homely, no longer young.
His speech had an accent
but I could not place it
and supposed he had come to this country as a young man
and gone right to work.
''Certainly.''

''I have paper and an envelope—
two if you spoil one.''
He smiled, took note paper and an envelope out of his pocket,
and we went to one of the desks in the post-office,
and I picked up a pen.
The letter was to go to a girl named Sadie,

111

somewhere in a small town
in Connecticut or Pennsylvania.
I wrote the full name and address on the envelope
as he watched me.
"Now what shall I write?"

"Dear Sadie," he began, "I love you.
Got that?" "Yes. Next."
"I love you."
"You said that. What next?"
"I love you. Write it again."
"All right. Next?"
"I love you."
I looked at him. "Have you nothing else to say?"
"Yes."
He thought a while and said:
"I love you very much. Got it?"
"Yes."
"Now write—." I was tempted to say,
I love you,
but I didn't want to make fun of him.
"Write: Please excuse me, Sadie."

"You see," he said, turning to me,
"she went out with another man
and I call her, 'Bitch! Whore!'
Now she do not want to see me.
Write: Please excuse me, Sadie. I love you."

I thought of a plain bird with only two or three notes
piping away on a tree in winter.

[115]

When I came for my laundry, I found a shirt missing.
The laundryman—a Jew—considered the situation:
"There are four ways of losing a shirt," he said thoughtfully;
"in the first place, it may never have been delivered by the steam
     laundry;
in the second place, it may be lying around here, unpacked;
in the third place, it may have been delivered and packed in
     someone else's bundle;
and in the fourth place it may be really lost.
Come in again at the end of the week and I'll know what has
     happened."
And his wife, recognizing a fellow Jew,
smiled and spoke up in Yiddish,
"We won't have to go to the rabbi about it, will we?"

[116]

The new janitor is a Puerto Rican;
still a young man and he has four small children.
He has been hired because he is cheap—
not because he is the handy man
a good janitor is supposed to be.
I doubt if he ever saw any plumbing
before he came to this country,
to say nothing of a boiler and radiators.
Anyway, he was soon overwhelmed by requests from the tenants
to do this and fix that.
He does his best and spends hours at simple jobs,
and seldom does them well—or can do them at all.

He was in my flat once
to do something or other and, when he was through,
asked me if he might sit down.

"Of course," I said and offered him a drink,
but he would not take it.
"It is so quiet here," he explained.
And then he began to talk about a man who lived in the house and
     taught Spanish.
"He talks to me in Spanish," the janitor said,
"but I do not understand.
You see, I am not an educated man."
His eye caught the print of a water-color by Winslow Homer
which I have hanging: a palm tree in the Bahamas.
"That is my country," he said,
and kept looking at the print
as one might look at a photograph of one's mother
long dead.

[117]

The Chinese girl in the waiting-room of the busy railway station
writing on a pad
in columns
as if she were adding figures
instead of words—
words in blue ink
that look like small flowers
stylized into squares:
she is planting a small private garden.

[118]

The dark subway-station was almost empty at a little after ten
that summer morning. The man who sold tokens for the turnstiles
was going back to his booth with a broad smile on his face.

114

I supposed he had been engaged in an amusing conversation
with the Negro alone on the platform.
The black man's face was wrinkled. As he stood there,
stooped over a stick, he kept on talking:
"I cuss my mother in her grave," he was saying in a loud angry
    voice,
"because she borned me!"
What a line for a "Mammy" song, I thought.
By this time there were two or three other passengers on the
    platform
and we stood at a distance from the Negro and watched him,
though we pretended not to. He turned to us and said,
"I wonder how it feels to be white."

Just then the train came in and we went inside
hoping that the Negro with his disturbance
would not enter the brightly-lit car.

[119]

I saw him walking along slowly at night
holding a tray of candy and chewing-gum:
a Jewish boy of fifteen or sixteen
with large black eyes and gentle face.
He sidled into a saloon
and must have been ordered away
because he came out promptly
through the swinging doors.

I wondered what he was doing
far from a Jewish neighborhood.
(I knew the side streets
and the roughs standing about on the corners and stoops.)

115

What a prize this shambling boy with his tray!
I stepped up to warn him
against leaving the brightly-lit avenue.
He listened, eyed me steadily, and walked on calmly.
I looked at him in astonishment
and thought: has nothing frightened you?
Neither the capture of Jerusalem by the Babylonians, by the
    Romans, by the Crusaders?
No pogrom in Russia;
no Nazi death-camp in Germany?
How can you still go about so calmly?

[120]

I was wearing a belt buckle
with the initial of my family name on it
in a cheap design. A friend noticed it
and I said apologetically:
"This was my father's. He had no taste."
"Perhaps," my friend answered gently,
"he wore it because it was a gift."

[121]

A sign on a store window: no fancy name—just "Mrs. Smith's
    Cafeteria";
come in, if you like.
The street was dingy, the houses small and shabby,
but it was not a side street,
not a quiet street, by any means.
Streetcars and buses, motorcars and motor trucks,
ran along it all day long

until late at night, and it was lined with stores.
The stores were small, the merchandise cheap;
clearly a street where poor people walked and shopped.

The window was clean; in the window, a canary bird in a bright
    gilt cage—
nothing else.
Two or three men were eating at the small tables
and two or three waiting at the counter;
behind it an old woman—
she must surely have been seventy—
hair white as the chinaware,
small and hunchbacked with age,
and alone.
Serving everybody and everything—
the meat or fish, the vegetables,
white bread or corn bread, the salad, dessert and coffee or milk;
and she took the money, too,
brought a glass of water to the table when the customer was seated,
and carried off the dirty dishes.

The food was plain and cheap. She filled each order quickly
before a customer changed his mind—if he was that sort;
nothing dropped from her fork or spoon
as she lifted it to the plate;
the water did not slop over as she put the glass on the table;
there was no fumbling. She kept them waiting, of course,
as she briskly served each customer in turn,
but she made no apology, wasted no words.
What do you wish, young man? Young woman?—
they were all young as they stood before her—
choose and pay,
then eat and dawdle as much as you like;
but I have no time to dilly-dally;
I am old and alone.

During the Second World War, I was going home one night
along a street I seldom used. All the stores were closed
except one—a small fruit store.
An old Italian was inside to wait on customers.
As I was paying him I saw that he was sad.
"You are sad," I said. "What is troubling you?"
"Yes," he said, "I am sad." Then he added
in the same monotone, not looking at me:
"My son left for the front today and I'll never see him again."
"Don't say that!" I said. "Of course, you will!"
"No," he answered. "I'll never see him again."

Afterwards, when the war was over,
I found myself once more in that street
and again it was late at night, dark and lonely;
and again I saw the old man alone in the store.
I bought some apples and looked closely at him:
his thin wrinkled face was grim
but not particularly sad. "How about your son?" I said.
"Did he come back from the war?" "Yes," he answered.
"He was not wounded?" "No. He is all right."
"That's fine," I said. "Fine!"
He took the bag of apples from my hands and groping inside
took out one that had begun to rot
and put in a good one instead.
"He came back at Christmas," he added.
"How wonderful! That was wonderful!"
He took the bag of apples from my hands again
and took out one of the smaller apples and put in a large one.

[123]

In the street, nine stories below, the horn of an automobile out of
    order
began sounding its loudest
steadily—without having to stop for breath.
We tried to keep on talking
in spite of that unceasing scream;
raised our voices somewhat, no longer calm and serene.
Our civilization was somewhat out of order, it seemed.

But, just as we began to knit our brows,
tighten our jaws, twist our lips,
the noise stopped;
and we dipped our heads,
like ducks on a stream, into the cool silence,
and talked again quietly, smiling at each other.

[124]

A cold wind was blowing down the street in gusts;
the streetlamps were merely threads and points of light.
In the morning my mind had been like a spool of cotton;
now all the thread had been stitched away at my job
and only the wooden spool was left.

The straight street really went up and down in waves of asphalt,
and only the tired walker knew
how often it rose into the teeth of the wind.

[125]

When a child of four or five,
I would sit beside the rubber plant at night
if unable to sleep;
the stiff starched curtain pushed aside.
The lights were out in the stores
and the street, in spite of the arc-lamps,
dark and still.
After a while the trolley wire would begin to hum and sing
in the darkness
until the trolley itself rushed past,
ablaze with light.

Content
at the periphery of such wonder
I would lean back in the chair
to wait patiently for the next car.

[126]

My father's parents were a strange pair:
my grandmother tall, even for a man,
and she walked, when more than seventy,
straight and stiff as a grenadier;
a good-looking woman with strong regular features
and bright blue eyes.
My grandfather was no taller than five feet—
if that much:
in the Ukrainian village where he had lived most of his life,
his fellow Jews used to call him,
because of his size, ''Simon the Flea.''
He was timid, too, when I knew him,

and would walk along the street with a glance, now and then,
behind him
as if he were waiting for a stone to come flying at his head.
No doubt many had.

When my grandfather was a boy,
perhaps no more than six or seven,
his father had jumped into the water of the neighboring river—
swollen with melting ice and snow in the spring,
it had overflowed its banks and was sweeping away the stalls of the
        marketplace—
to save an old woman from drowning.
He took sick with pneumonia because of this
and died.
His son, now that he was an orphan,
never had enough to eat
or a decent place where to sleep,
and did well enough to grow up at all.
But in the synagogue the orphan found himself
at ease in Zion,
and, in the teaching of the rabbis,
became more than the equal of many a man.
Men spoke well of him;
and my grandmother's father, somewhat of a scholar himself,
thought he could find no better husband
for his tall pretty daughter, now all of fifteen.
Since she had no say in the matter,
married she was
to this little timid lad,
so unlike the strapping peasants
and even the Jews of her village.

My grandfather had a great deal of trouble earning a living
at first,

but in time God blessed him,
as He had blessed Abraham, Isaac, and Jacob.
Although never the butcher himself,
he bought cattle and sold beef,
and became the richest, as he was the most learned, Jew of his
    village.
However, his wife's temper and tongue
became proverbial.
My mother used to explain this
by saying that her mother-in-law had little love for learning;
but my grandmother knew how to read and write better than most
    women of her kind
and, when she was old and had a little time for herself at last,
she found pleasure in reading.

When my grandfather was about fifty, he fell sick,
and my grandparents thought it best to go to America
where my father and their other children were.
My father went to the pier to bring his parents to our home
and could hardly recognize his father—
the face was swollen
and the man could hardly move his hands and feet.
I had been watching from the window
and my brother and I ran downstairs
to meet them. My father turned to my grandfather
and said: "These are my sons."
My grandfather looked at us with his bleary eyes,
whose rims were red,
and turning to my father murmured in Hebrew
what the patriarch Jacob had said to his son Joseph:
"I did not think to see your face
and God has shown me your sons also,"
and, putting his swollen hands slowly on my head,
began to bless me. Even as he did so,

my grandmother who was standing beside him
poked him in the ribs and said sharply in Yiddish:
"Well?"
My grandfather hurriedly brought the blessing to a close.
Shoving his fist into his pocket he took out a gold coin
and put it in the hand I had stretched out to greet him.
"No, no," I said
and would have given the coin back,
for I had been brought up to think it disgraceful
to take money from my elders: the purpose of the instruction
was that I should not ask for pennies,
as ill-bred children did; in good Talmudical style
the prohibition was wider than the evil.
But this time my father smiled and said:
"Keep it—to remember your grandfather by."
As they went into the house,
I stopped to glance at the coin
and saw the monstrous eagle of czarist Russia,
with two open beaks,
from which my father and mother and so many others had fled.

[127]

There was a small settlement-house near where we lived
and I became friendly with two of the boys I met there—
Eugene and Gabriel, children of Hungarian Jews.
The three of us had this in common:
we liked to write
which for us then, still in high school, meant mostly reading.
Eugene's father had a store in which he sold flannel shirts and
      woolen underwear to firemen.
Years before, he had peddled them about the fire-houses of the
      city.

123

No doubt, he had then to put up with a good deal of joking,
for he was a small, homely man, and a Jew at that.
When I knew him, he had authority in his voice
and dignity in his bearing,
and was respected by his customers—and tenants,
for he owned several tenements in the neighborhood
and these were kept as clean and orderly as his store.
If the day was sunny, I would usually find Eugene sitting in front
      of it.
While his father spread the flannel along the counter for the shirts
      he sold,
layer on layer, and cut it according to the patterns,
Eugene and I, outside, would be talking about poetry,
especially the poetry of the new men—new to us—
Francis Thompson, Arthur Symons, and Ernest Dowson.
This was not in our English course,
and Eugene and I felt superior because we read them,
and were proud of ourselves because we, too, were writing verse,
and trying our hands at sonnets
and the French confectionary Austin Dobson—for one—was good
      at.

Gabriel was older than either of us—
a sarcastic fellow. But he knew much more than I
and was so generous of all he knew
that I listened humbly and did not mind his smiles and quiet gibes.
He had read much verse,
chiefly the Elizabethans and the metaphysical poets,
and their nimble speech delighted him.
His own verse, merely gymnastics of his own quick mind,
was full of sudden twists of thought—
balancing itself on the necessity of rhyme and a strict meter.
He prided himself on how fast he could dash it off
and never kept anything of what he wrote,

except as he happened to remember some of it,
and seldom gave it a second thought.
His parents, unlike Eugene's, were poor
and lived in a dingy house—in a dingy flat.
From the back of it, I could see the yards unevenly paved
and the multitudinous windows of tenements
and many clotheslines, always hung with washing.
Sometimes his mother—or stepmother—a stout sad-faced woman,
would come out of a dark bedroom,
which had neither door nor window and only a hanging in the
        doorway,
at the sound of our cheerful voices;
or would leave the front room, where she sat at a window watching
        the mean street below,
to look at us and go back without a word.
I would see Gabriel's father, too, at times:
a stout man, shabbily dressed,
who spoke briefly to his wife in a low voice
and never to his son while I was there.
I guessed that he had a pushcart,
or did something even humbler like peddling from a basket;
for his son, in spite of a smile when he spoke of his father's work,
seemed anxious to hide it.

Gabriel showed me where to buy second-hand books,
and on Saturdays we would walk from stall to stall.
It was no use looking at books that cost a quarter or more—
for we seldom had more than a couple of dimes to spend—
but still we managed to buy many a dusty, ill-smelling volume.
We handled many books of sermons and many of verse;
looked at each patiently,
for among the sermons we might find those of Latimer or even
        Donne—
although we never did—

and we dipped into each book of verse,
for of course we knew that Rossetti or Swinburne had found the
    Rubaiyat
in just such a pile.
One Saturday, Gabriel bought a copy of the Greek Anthology—
in Greek, for he could read it—
and I found in a single volume all the English poets
from Ben Jonson to Beattie.
It had been bound in brown morocco, but only one board
    remained,
and the pages had yellow spots.
Still, the small print was clear
and, as the ''advertisement'' or introduction said,
''all the classical English poets'' were there.
Few poems, no matter in how many cantos, were left out,
except those ''unsuited to the perusal of youth.''
This, no doubt, more than the damaged binding and spotted pages
had condemned it to lie among the cheapest books.
And on this fortunate day, to the envy of Gabriel,
who had taught me to admire Sartain's deep shading and thin
    lines,
I had also found a book with more than twenty of his engravings.
(Gabriel praised much others held cheap—
only, so he thought, because of their stupidity.)
With our new possessions
we walked slowly down the sunny avenue
to Gabriel's home. As we did so,
a ship, keeping time with us, went smoothly down the river,
hull hidden, but masts and sails showing
above the gutter of each street we crossed.

We had our supper in the large kitchen—
a roll each and coffee. The coffee was mostly chicory with hot
    milk,

which I did not care for,
but the roll was fresh and hot and the sweet butter on it very good.
Afterwards, as we each sat by a window
and looked out into the bright world—
for it was still daylight—
we set ourselves to writing sonnets on a given theme.
We knew that Keats and Leigh Hunt used to do that.
I had Gabriel choose the theme,
for this was to be a test of my skill in writing verse
as against his. He finished long before I did.
It had become twilight,
but there was still light enough to read what we had written.
Gabriel's sonnet was something fantastic,
which I did not care for; but he said that he liked mine—
and, indeed, I liked it very much.

One evening, when I had not seen Gabriel in years,
and we had become men with serious and unpleasant work to do
        for our living,
I was on a station where the subway ran above ground
in a neighborhood to which I went seldom.
It was late at night
and the train was long in coming.
The cold open air was pleasanter than the foul air of the waiting-
        room
and I walked about, lost in thought,
and listened to my steps crunching the newly-fallen snow.
It lay an inch thick on the narrow wooden planking
beyond the cement platform. At the very end of the station
I came upon Gabriel, under a bright light:
the slack body and the small head with yellow hair and green eyes.
There was a rather pretty woman with him;
they were talking together familiarly
and yet without any great interest in what each was saying,

as husband and wife at times talk to each other.
He looked at me for a moment coldly
and then shifted his eyes;
and I turned slowly
and stood at a distance waiting for the train.

[128]

I went to my grandfather's to say good-bye:
I was going away to a school out West.
As I came in,
my grandfather turned from the window at which he sat
(sick, skin yellow, eyes bleary—
but his hair still dark,
for my grandfather had hardly any grey hair in his beard
        or on his head—
he would sit at the window, reading a Hebrew book).
He rose with difficulty—
he had been expecting me, it seemed—
stretched out his hands and blessed me in a loud voice:
in Hebrew, of course,
and I did not know what he was saying.
When he had blessed me,
my grandfather turned aside and burst into tears.
"It is only for a little while, Grandpa," I said
in my broken Yiddish. "I'll be back in June."
(By June my grandfather was dead.)
He did not answer.
Perhaps my grandfather was in tears for other reasons:
perhaps, because, in spite of all the learning I had acquired
        in high school,
I knew not a word of the sacred text of the Torah
and was going out into the world

with none of the accumulated wisdom of my people to guide me,
with no prayers with which to talk to the God of my people,
a soul—
for it is not easy to be a Jew or, perhaps, a man—
doomed by his ignorance to stumble and blunder.

[129]

I now went to law school in the evening.
The instruction was by reading cases—
no lectures that stuffed pap into the mouth of the student;
and we soon learned, under the incitement of our teachers,
to question—if questioning was called for—
the opinion of each case
and, perhaps, that of our teachers.
Most of my fellow students were older than I
and earnest (almost all worked during the day
in factories or in law offices),
and their questions had steel in them;
unlike the students in the morning or afternoon classes,
mostly just out of high school
and too timid to speak or, if they did,
poked feeble questions
like the sticks that children use as swords.
At first I read more poetry than cases,
but then threw myself zestfully
into the dog fight that each period became
and, to be ready for it,
learned to probe beneath the facts of each case
for the living principle of law
and to trace it, if I could,
to the solid trunk from which it sprang;
confused as it all was to me at first,

I soon saw the law in its elements as a beautiful order
in which benefit balanced obligation
and nothing was without its reason—or reasons.

The law that we studied
was not always the actual law
of judges or statutes
but an ideal—
from which new branches were ever springing
as society became complicated
and the new rights of its individuals clear.
I found it delightful
to climb those green heights,
to bathe in the clear waters of reason,
to use words for their daylight meaning
and not as prisms
playing with the rainbows of connotation:
after the dim lights, the colored phrases, the cloying music,
the hints of what the poets meant
and did not quite say
(for to suggest was to create
and to name was to destroy—
according to the Symbolists, at least),
the plain sunlight of the cases,
the sharp prose,
the forthright speech of the judges;
it was good, too, to stick my mind against the sentences of a judge,
and drag the meaning out of the shell of words.
And when our teacher of contracts,
who was also the dean of the school,
produced a theory of acceptance
(which was not actually the law anywhere),
I was delighted, walking along the streets deep in thought,
to find a flaw in the theory

and boldly produce another, my very own—
to find that I, too, could think like a lawyer.

I soon had no time for writing or reading anything but law
and spent my days in the law library
diligently reading cases and memorizing sentences that seemed
    meaty;
reading each page as often as I liked
with nothing to jog my elbow or step on my heel;
sifting the facts of each case until I had only the hard essentials;
underlining words and phrases
until I had plotted the judge's reasoning;
and digging for the bedrock of law on which the cases stood—
or did not stand.
The noise of the street was far away—
ten storeys below;
far away, too, the worry and noise of my parents' shop;
before me was all that was left of eager argument and eager parties,
now merely names that might just as well have been,
and in the talk of the law students often were,
single letters of the alphabet:
all the blood—the heartache and the heartening—gone out of the
    words
and only, as a pattern for thinking,
the cool bones of the judge's reasoning.
And I felt no regret for the glittering words I had played with
and only pleasure to be working with ideas—
of rights and wrongs and their elements
and of justice between men in their intricate affairs.

The last class was over at ten.
I would try to get home before midnight
and had to walk briskly to do it:
a mile or two to the bridge

through streets now mostly empty and still;
over the bridge again,
often meeting with nobody for the whole mile of it,
especially if the wind was cold or when it would snow or rain;
and then the long walk in Brooklyn, five or six miles,
the streets quiet and dark and the neighborhood of my home
quietest of all—
lawns and gardens, a park and empty lots.

Suddenly all delight in my studies was gone—
melted with the snow in the spring.
True enough, the studies of the second year were less interesting
than those of the first:
less probing after principle and more of practice,
less general reasoning and more of statutory requirement,
necessary enough but detailed and dull;
but what bothered me most, unlooked for
and against will and reason,
with the suddenness of a fever,
was the longing to write:
as if all that I had seen and heard and remembered
and, for the most part, felt only slightly,
was not gone, as I had thought,
but stored in a reservoir
that now, filled to the brim, was overrunning—
pouring over on all sides.
(It was, of course, no reservoir, but only a kettleful—
but it had come to a boil.)
And here I was, busied with this tiresome study of the law,
these tiring studies that left me no time
and, if time, no strength
to write. My bulky lawbooks had become, over night,
too heavy to lift and the cases palaver.

I had been bothered by a secret weariness
with meter and regular stanzas
grown a little stale. The smooth lines and rhymes
seemed to me affected, a false stress on words and syllables—
fake flowers
in the streets in which I walked.
and yet I found prose
without the burst of song and the sudden dancing—
without the intensity which I wanted.
The brand-new verse some Americans were beginning to write—
after the French "free verse," perhaps,
or the irregular rhythms of Walt Whitman,
the English translations of the Hebrew Bible
and, earlier yet, the rough verse of the Anglo-Saxons—
seemed to me, when I first read it,
right:
not cut to patterns, however cleverly,
nor poured into ready molds,
but words and phrases flowing as the thought;
to be read just as common speech
but for stopping at the turn of each line—
and this like a rest in music or a turn in the dance.
(I found it no criticism that to read such verse as prose
was to have a kind of prose,
for that was not to read it as it was written.)
And with the even artificial beat of the old meters,
I gave up the artifice of rhyme:
not only because I had the authority of Milton
and the usage of the Elizabethans in their plays;
I liked a Doric music better.
Now, too, I became friendly with one my own age,
whom I had met the summer before
thinking him just another acquaintance.
Al proved to be as helpful as my new reading.

He had come to see me at my home that summer
about to teach in the West where I had studied
five years before
that I might tell him of the place;
I had little to say and he listened
almost indifferently,
smiling half in friendship and half mockingly,
hardly looking at me with his bright blue eyes.
When he was back next summer for his vacation,
with nothing better to do, perhaps,
he came to see me again
but now we had the new verse to talk of.
I showed him what of mine had been taken for publication
in a new magazine for verse only;
but he read my verse as I had never read verse before,
scrutinizing it, phrase by phrase
and word by word, thought and image, thought and sound;
and much, if not all, that had seemed good to me
now had the dead sound of a counterfeit
on his marble good sense.
That was the way he had read Shakespeare at college—
without such effect, of course—
and so, except that I gave little thought
to image or sound,
was how I had read my law cases.
But, in spite of my early dislike of journalism
because of its hurried and careless writing,
I used to write verse just as carelessly—
as it flew into my head.
Now doing just what Al did,
I saw that I could use the expensive machinery
that had cost me four years of hard work at law
and which I had thought useless for my writing:
prying sentences open to look at the exact meaning:

weighing words to choose only those that had meat for my purpose
and throwing the rest away as empty shells.
I, too, could scrutinize every word and phrase
as if in a document or the opinion of a judge
and listen, as well, for tones and overtones,
leaving only the pithy, the necessary, the clear and plain.

Al read nothing on his knees,
and delighted in finding out for himself
what made a poem or story tick—
if it did. We began to spend much time together,
our spirits swaggering about,
blaming and praising each other's writing,
as well as that of the rest of the world—
"we poets whose lives begin in gladness."
Perhaps, if all our eager talk had been written down,
some of it would have seemed, afterwards,
as jejune as comments an arrogant self
had written in the margin of books
in those proud days when I read with a pencil.
But not all. We might, for example, talk about the story from the
        Japanese
that Lafcadio Hearn used. A man is lost in the woods.
It is going to storm. Anxious to ask his way,
he hurries up to what he takes for a peasant,
walking ahead of him in the gathering darkness.
The peasant—or whatever it is he is talking to—
turns
and the traveler sees a face without nose or eyes,
smooth as an egg, and rushes off.
Then, as he runs, stumbling, anxious now only to get away,
he sees again what he takes to be a peasant walking ahead of him.
He runs up, eager for any human companionship
after that earlier sight,

and blurts out what he has just seen;
and the same face turns to him again and asks:
''Was it anything like this?''
I might have said that the story was moving
because it meant that we should meet again
the horrible we thought we had escaped,
or that our secret terrors warn us
of what we shall surely face. Al said:
''Compare this with a German fairy tale.
When the Germans want to make a figure horrible,
a witch, for instance,
they enlarge the eyes, lengthen the nose, the teeth, the nails—
they add, they exaggerate;
but the Japanese make a more horrible figure
because less human:
they take everything away—nose, mouth, and even eyes.''

I reread my verse that had been taken for publication
and found much in so few lines to change or strike out
and wrote the magazine about it,
but the editor assured me, of the longer poem,
that it was meant—
by Apollo, no doubt—
to be in quatrains, as first written,
and that the irregularities with which I proposed to remedy the
        verse
only spoiled it.
However, if changes were in order,
she suggested a number off-hand
and these I could not see at all.
In the meantime, I had sent her more verse,
of which she took another poem
to add to the two to be published,

but would not have one or two I thought the best—
better than any of mine she had taken.
The other magazines, to judge by what they were printing,
were not even worth bothering with, I thought,
with the arrogance of the young:
and for the judgment of the editor who was to print my verse
I had, by this time,
little respect.
Besides, publication in a magazine, pleasant as it would be,
seemed less important than perfection,
at least whatever degree of it I could reach.
And, as I thought about it,
it seemed to me that if I could accustom myself to working at my
        verse daily,
revising until I had a group to my own satisfaction,
and could have group after group printed,
I might in time, say, in a lifetime,
have a few poems——
the quintessence of all I had to say.
But I could not, it seemed to me,
just put my verse away in a drawer until the Messiah should come;
for the impulse to write—in which I had such pleasure—
and, above all, to revise wholeheartedly,
would be, perhaps would have to be, stimulated
by regular publication.
And again, revision year after year,
of what I might have lying about
unpublished,
would become destructive merely,
rubbing out much that by constant review
would seem unnecessary
and had become tiresome.
Publication in a magazine, such as was now promised,
of a couple of poems now and then—

even as I would have them—
hardly seemed worth while.
But, since I did not hope for a publisher
to print my verse soon at his own risk
and I did not have the money to pay for a publisher's imprint—
nor did I relish the pretence—
why, I thought, I should print privately,
that is, pay the printer and make no pretence of having a publisher
    at all.
There was little notice to be had that way, I knew,
among the crowd of new books;
but, besides the stimulation to write and revise,
I would clear my head and heart
for new work. Yes, the work was the thing.
Large circulation is pleasant, of course,
but I did not find it necessary:
as if one has seen something exciting in the street
he must tell it—
perhaps because man is communicative—
but, after he has told his vision
once or twice,
handed on his knowledge to two or three,
he is free to go about his other business.

Besides, the urgency of war (for the country was now in the First
    World War)
made it seem advisable to arrange my affairs;
and, since my affairs were verse,
to put it, slight though in bulk and value, in order
and leave it printed behind me;
for I doubted that anyone else
would go to that trouble and any expense.
I knew two stories to strengthen me in my resolution—
one I had read and the other my mother told me:

Balzac's story of the painter who kept working at his painting
until when seen at last it was only a mass of paint,
except for a beautiful hand
which showed what the painting might have been—
this for the danger in endless revision;
and my mother's story of her father
who became a kind of broker
making his little commissions on sales of cattle or wheat
and beguiled his spirit as he wandered about the countryside
writing verse in Hebrew—
until he suddenly died of influenza far from home.
And when with his bundle of clothes there was brought back a
        sheaf of papers—
his verse, the writing of thirty years—
my grandmother burnt every scrap of it, dearly as she loved him;
for fear that the writing which she could not read
or, if she could, did not understand,
might send her children to jail
should any of it be construed as treasonable against the Czar.
Well, I would leave no writing of mine,
if I could help it,
to the mercy of those who loved me.
I would print
and, though I knew it was an unlikely way to gain name or money
(not that I cared much for either),
I also knew a Chinese proverb
that one who can work ten years without recognition
will be known everywhere,
and the tradition in English verse of private publication
as the "Rubaiyat" was published and "Leaves of Grass."
Later, when I was to have much time and a little money,
I learnt how to print;
indeed, setting type by hand and running a platen-press by foot
is not too hard:

the great wheel turning, the rollers moving down over the sticky
    black platen,
shining arms sliding smoothly into their grooves
and the type closing on the blank paper—
to leave a printed sheet.
I would stop the wheel at each revolution,
unable to feed the press as a printer could
but, slow as I was, I would print four hundred sheets in a couple of
    hours—
more than enough.
A difficulty was room for the heavy press.
I had it in the basement of my parents' house;
when they moved, the press was dismantled,
coated with oil, stored, and finally sold—and lost.

[131]

EPILOGUE

The rest is like the manna of the Israelites
which, gathered into their baskets,
made a great heap
but did not outlast the day.

Jews in Babylonia

(uncollected, 1969)

[132]

JEWS IN BABYLONIA*

I

1

Plough, sow and reap,
thresh and winnow
in the season of the wind;
a woman is grinding wheat
or baking bread.
In the third watch of the night
the child sucks from the breast of its mother
and the woman talks with her husband.

Plough, sow and reap,
bind the sheaves, thresh and winnow;

*Collages based for the most part on translations from the Talmud.

141

shear the sheep,
wash the wool,
comb it and weave it.

Wheat and barley,
straw and stubble;
the cock crows, the horse neighs, and the ass brays;
an ox is grazing in a meadow or straying on the road
or rubbing itself against a wall
(a black ox for its hide,
a red one for its flesh,
and a white one for plowing);

plough, sow, cut, bind, thresh, winnow, and set up a stack.

2

A cow to plough with
and an ass to drive;
a goat for milking
and an ewe for shearing.

A hen for laying eggs
and a date tree for its fruit;
a bed on which to sit
and a table at which to eat.

3

Plane the wood
into boards;
chisel the stones;
beat the wool and bleach it,
spin it and weave it.

A beast with its load
and a bit in its mouth
and a bell on its neck;
an ass with its bundle of wood
and a camel with a load of flax and an iron nose-ring
or a horse with bells between its eyes;
the horn gores,
the hoof kicks,
the teeth bite.

4

The bread has become moldy
and the dates blown down by the wind;
the iron has slipped from the helve.
The wool was to be dyed red
but the dyer dyed it black.

The dead woman has forgotten her comb
and tube of eye-paint;
the dead cobbler has forgotten his knife,
the dead butcher his chopper,
and the dead carpenter his adze.

A goat can be driven off with a shout.
But where is the man to shout?
The bricks pile up, the laths are trimmed,
and the beams are ready. Where is the builder?

To be buried in a linen shroud
or in a matting of reeds—
but where are the dead of the Flood
and where the dead of Nebuchadnezzar?

1

Palm trees in a valley
and reeds beside the bed of a stream:
a caravan camped in the valley, surrounded by camels,
saddles, saddle cushions and saddle bags.
The dried leaves of a palm for fuel
or, tied together, to sit on.

A walled town with Jews:
houses with balconies on courtyards
and a porter's lodge at each gate;
a market square with stalls and shutters,
the synagogue and bath-house.

Flowing rivers and gushing springs,
the tide of the sea,
and water dripping from the roof.

2

The old man may have forgotten most of what he knew
but even the fragments of the broken Tables of the Law
were kept—out of respect—in the Ark.

3

As when a girl with smooth shining yellow hair
comes into a room where three young men are hard at work
and all three look up smiling joyfully.

4

When her father walked from his house to the House of Study,

his servants spread woolen cloths before his feet,
and the poor who followed rolled them up and took them away;
now his daughter is picking barley grains in the dung of Arab
    cattle,
looking for barley grains among the hoofs of the horses.

5

A purple cloak and a white horse with a red bridle
and the black walls of the charcoal-burner;
clothing of cloth, of leather, or of sacking;
eating coarse bread instead of fine,
drinking new wine instead of old,
and sleeping on straw instead of in a soft bed,
but, rejoicing at your lot,
you are rich.

6

If the ship you are traveling on is wrecked,
a plank may come floating your way;
and on it you may ride wave after wave
until you walk again on dry land.

III

1

The rock is hard
but iron splits it;
iron is hard
but fire softens it;
fire is strong

145

but water quenches it—
and the clouds carry the water away
and the wind scatters them.

2

The hyena will turn into a bat
and a bat into a thorn.

3

The dog eats the lamb and a cat the hens,
and lions fill their dens with prey.

4

The blood of his wounds
and the tears of her eyes.

The Angel of Death in time of war
does not distinguish
between the righteous and the wicked.

5

If you cannot look at the sun—
only one of God's ministers—
how can you see God Himself?

IV

1

Clap hands and slap your thighs;
adding indulgence to indulgence, sin to sin,
the thread of the spider becomes a rope.

2

Only bones and nut shells left on the table.
Degenerate son;
vinegar, son of wine!

3

They praise each other;
like whores
painting one another.

V

I kill and I quicken;
I wound and I heal;
I speak out of the whirlwind
and a thorn bush.
When the earth was still a waste
without grass or tree, bird and beast,
I was; and when the earth will be a waste again
without bird or man—
I am.

The sun shines
and the rain falls;

all are equal before Me—
man and beast alike:

those treading the winepress or bringing in sheaves;
the merchants and their porters
and those coming into town to sell from wicker baskets;
the rich man feeling for his purse
and he who sits before a scroll of the Law
written with a fine reed-pen and by a skilled penman;
the shepherd with his wallet
and the blind man with his staff—
with a torch at night
not to see but to be seen;
the dryer of figs; the quarryman and the man who smoothes and
    polishes the stones;
the night watchman, the watchman of a cucumber bed,
and the man guarding his fruit against birds
or his gourds against wild beasts,
clapping his hands or stamping his foot;
the ass-driver and the camel-driver,
those with boots muddied by clay;
and those who walk between thorns and thistles, thorns and briers;

the bull and bullock, calf, ram and lamb, kid or goat;
cat and marten, and the squeaking mice,
the cackling hens, doves hopping about,
and the fowl scratching on a dung-heap;
the ravens screaming and screeching,
falcon or hawk,
the wolf, the lion, bear, leopard, panther and the snake,
the flies, the gnats and worms—
even the worms eating away at the scrolls of the Law—
and the mites of grapes,
the locusts, serpents and scorpions:

all are equal before Me;

all the creatures that live in the sea
and those that live upon the dry land,
and the creatures that live in the air
and those that live in fire.

From

Holocaust

(unpublished, 1973)

HOLOCAUST*

THE NARRATOR

The National Socialist German Workers Party, known as the Nazis, took over Germany in January, 1933. Their policy at first was merely to force the Jews to emigrate. By 1941, this policy was changed to extermination of the Jews, not only in Germany but in all countries the Nazis annexed, invaded or dominated. It has been estimated that six million Jews lost their lives: about four and a half million in Poland and in the invaded parts of Russia.

[133]

THE WITNESS

We are the civilized—

*All that follows is based on a United States government publication, *Trials of the Criminals before the Nuernberg Tribunal.* and the records of the Eichmann trial in Jerusalem.

Aryans;
and do not always kill those condemned to death
merely because they are Jews
as the less civilized might:
we use them to benefit science
as if they were rats or mice:
to find out the limits of human endurance
at the highest altitudes
for the good of the German air force;
force them to stay in tanks of ice water
or naked outdoors for hours and hours
at temperatures below freezing;
yes, study the effects of going without food
and drinking only sea water
for days and days
for the good of the German navy;
or wound them and force wooden shavings or ground glass
into the wounds,
or take out bones, muscles and nerves,
or burn their flesh—
to study the burns caused by bombs—
or put poison in their food
or infect them with malaria, typhus, or other fevers—
all for the good of the German army.
Heil Hitler!

[134]

THE WITNESS

A number of Jews had to drink sea water only
to find out how long they could stand it.
In their torment

152

they threw themselves on the mops and rags
used by the hospital attendants
and sucked the dirty water out of them
to quench the thirst
driving them mad.

[135]

THE WITNESS

Jewish women were lined up by German troops in charge of the
    invaded territory,
told to undress,
and they stood in their undergarments.
An officer, looking at the row of women,
stopped to look at a young woman—
tall, with long braided hair, and wonderful eyes.
He kept looking at her, then smiled and said,
"Take a step forward."
Dazed—as they all were—she did not move
and he said again: "Take a step forward!
Don't you want to live?"
She took that step
and then he said: "What a pity
to bury such beauty in the earth.
Go!
But don't look backwards.
There is the street to the boulevard.
Follow that."
She hesitated
and then began to walk as told.
The other women looked at her—
some no doubt with envy—

153

as she walked slowly, step by step.
And the officer took out his revolver
and shot her in the back.

[136]

THE WITNESS

The officers in one camp, for their amusement,
if they saw a group of inmates at a distance,
would draw their revolvers and shoot in that direction;
but they must have shot into the air
because no one was ever hit.
Throwing stones at the group was another matter:
inmates would be hurt—in the face, hands or legs.
But, in another camp, the two commanders began a game:
they would stand at their windows
and, while those of the inmates carrying stones were passing,
the two would shoot at them, aiming at the tip of a nose or a
        finger;
and in the evening would pick out those who had been hit
and were no longer any good for work
and have them shot.
And in still another camp the officers had a kind of torture
which had an element of amusement for them—
"the spinning top":
the officers would place a stick in the ground—stand it up quite
        low—
and the man to be tortured would have to keep touching it with his
        right hand,
his left hand behind his back,
and keep turning around the stick,
and as he ran around he was beaten

and those beating him would shout, "Quicker! Quicker!"
The inmate tortured would have to go around at least ten times,
and after three or four times some would faint.

Once the commander of a camp had eight of the strongest among
    the Jews
placed in a large barrel of water,
saying that they did not look clean,
and they had to stand in this barrel naked for twenty-four hours.
In the morning, other prisoners had to cut away the ice:
the men were frozen to death.
In this camp—and in others also—
they had an orchestra of Jews
who had to play every morning and evening
and whenever inmates were taken to be shot.
In one such camp,
the orchestra had all of sixty men.

[137]

THE WITNESS

In the morning the Jews were lined up by an officer
and the officer told them:
"You are Jews, unworthy of life,
but are now supposed to work."
They were put upon trucks
and taken away to a forest
and set to digging.
After two or three spadefuls of earth,
the spade of one hit something hard,
and he saw that it was the head of a human being.
There was also a bad smell all around.

He stopped digging
and the officer in charge came towards him shouting:
"Why did you stop?
Didn't you know there are bodies buried here?"
He had opened a mass grave.

There were about ten thousand dead in that grave.
And after they had dug up the bodies
they were told to burn them.
Planks had been brought and beams—long and heavy.
The Germans also brought a grinding machine to grind the bones
and the ground bones would then be sieved
for the gold fillings of teeth.
The dust of the bones would then be spread over the fields,
and the smell was dreadful—
they could hardly breathe.

They kept on working three months
opening mass graves;
and opened eight or nine.
In one those digging saw a boy of two or three,
lying on his mother's body.
He had little white shoes on
and a little white jacket,
and his face was pressed against his mother's.

One grave would remain open for new corpses
coming all the time;
a truck would bring the bodies, still warm,
to be thrown into the grave—
naked as Adam and Eve:
Jewish men, many of them bearded, and Jewish women and
        children.
The graves they had opened would be refilled with earth

and they had to plant grass all over them;
as for the dead—
a thousand bodies would be put on a pyre;
and there were two pyres of bodies burning all the time.

[138]

THE WITNESS

Fishing boats, excursion boats, and any kind of boat
were mustered at the ports;
and the Jews were escorted to the coast by the Danes—
many of them students—
and ferried to safety in Sweden:
about six thousand Danish Jews were rescued
and only a few hundred captured by the Germans.

[139]

THE WITNESS

Later, in October of 1944, the S.S. men began to empty the camp at
    Chelmno
but a hundred Jews were ordered to stay behind to work.
The gas trucks went towards Kello,
and those who were left behind
began to take everything apart.
On Sundays there was no work
and Jews would be placed in a row:
each had a bottle on his head
and the S.S. men amused themselves by shooting at the bottles.
If a bottle was hit,

the man lived;
but if the bullet landed below,
well, the man had it.

On a night in January,
those who were working there
heard a truck at the gate.
It was opened and two S.S. men came in.
One had a flashlight and shouted at the Jews,
"Five men follow me!"
They were taken out and those left behind heard five shots.
Then the other S.S. man came in and shouted,
"Five more—out!"
After the fourth group of five had been taken out and shot,
the S.S. man came in again.
But one of those left behind
was hiding behind the door,
a knife in his hand.
He jumped on the S.S. man and stabbed him,
broke his flashlight,
and stabbed him again and again.
He was shot in the foot
but ran into the neighboring woods and escaped.

[140]

THE WITNESS

One Saturday, when he was thirteen,
he was taking a walk with his father in the ghetto of Lodz;
they heard shots
and saw people falling.
And then his father fell down, too:

he had been shot and killed.
He himself was caught and put on a truck
but begged the men who held him prisoner to let him go home
to tell his mother what had happened
and that he was to go away with them;
but all they answered was, "Shut up!"
(Afterwards, when he was taking out the gold teeth of the dead at
     Chelmno
and had to go through all sorts of files,
he saw a photograph of his mother in one of them.)

When those held on the trucks with him got off in Chelmno,
they were told to put their feet on chairs
and both feet were chained to each other.
The length of the chain was about fifteen inches
and they had trouble walking: just hopped;
and the chains were left on their feet at night, too.

The group he was in first
was told to clean a building that had been bombed
before they came,
and they found bones and skulls and arms and legs scattered about;
and learned, afterwards, that Jews who were sick had been
     gathered in the building
and then it had been blown up.
On the second day of their arrival,
an officer of the S.S. came and told them,
"If you cannot work tell me so;
and those who can't work will go out into the fresh air."
Nobody spoke up,
but he was back in a few days
and asked again, "Who can't work?"
And one among them said, "It's a little hard for me.
I should like to rest a while.

I would appreciate it."
And the S.S. officer answered,
"I can't send just one man out.
I must send a number out to rest a while."
So a number stepped out of line
and he said, "All right, come with me."
They followed him
and he told them to lie down
and shot them dead.

About two or three months after the lad's arrival,
transports of Jews
began to arrive—a great number.
When the first crematorium was ready,
people were loaded into the gas trucks—
about a hundred in each—
they had each been given a cake of soap and a towel
and told they were going to take a shower;
then the door of the truck would be tightly closed
and when the truck moved the gas would pour into it—
and they were killed.
Then the gold teeth and gold fillings would be taken out of their
        mouths
and the gold rings taken away:
the lad worked at that nearly all the time,
helping a subordinate officer whose name was Walter.

Every fortnight there was a selection from the group the lad was in.
They were asked how long they had been there
and if anyone answered he had been there eight days,
he was sent into the woods
and shot.
The lad himself was there three months,
but whenever he was asked how long he had been there

would answer, "Two days."
But finally the S.S. officer questioning him
began to swear at him in German
and said he was lying.
At that he began to cry,
and Walter came up to the officer and said something or other—
the lad didn't know just what—
and after that the officer left him alone.

Together with other Jewish workers
the lad was made to go through an exercise:
an officer would come on Saturdays
and would take four at a time out of a group of fifty
and say, "You see this finger?
If I move it this way, stand;
and if it moves that way,
lie down." It was up and down and up and down
until they were completely out of breath.
Finally, the officer took out his pistol
and shot those who did not stand up and were still lying down.

A Jew who had just come to the camp the day before
was set to work bringing corpses to the crematorium
and saw his sister's corpse among them.
In the evening he went to the garbage dump—
there was not a strong guard there—
and fled. It was not noticed just then.
He managed to take the chain from one of his feet
and reached the river;
but the non-Jew on the ferry
saw the chain on his other foot
and ran back to where there was a German guard
and said, "There's a Jew escaping!"
The guard went to the bank of the river, found and killed him.

That evening, the commander of the group he had been in came
    and told them,
"Everybody out!"
The man who had tried to escape was, of course, missing.
Then the commander said, "Four men out!"
and sent them to the place to which the body had been brought.
They brought the body back
and the commander said, "You see, he tried to escape."
Then Walter took the lad who was in the same group as the man
    who had tried to escape
and sent the lad to the camp of the S.S. guards
to scrub the floor. The officer above the commander in charge of
    the group
came and said, "Fifteen out!"
and took his pistol and killed them.
Then he said, "Do you know why I did it?
Because a man had run away.
And if any of you tries to run away,
I will kill you all."
When the lad came back, he was told they had been looking for
    him
to be one of the fifteen.

They began to disband the camp three months before the Russians
    came.
There were only about eighty Jews left.
One of the German officers came and said that forty would be taken
    to another camp:
they would be much better off than in Chelmno.
The forty were put on a truck—
and it went towards the woods.
When the truck came back, the lad was sent by one of the Jews in
    the camp
to look for a note in the truck:

the men who had been sent away had said that if they were sent to
    the woods
they would send those who were left behind a note—
and they did:
it was in Hebrew and all it read was: "To death."

The Jews who were left were set to dismantling the camp—
all the huts—
and in January the door of the hut they were in was suddenly
    opened
and a commander said, "Five out!"
The lad was among them.
There was a young doctor from Czechoslovakia among them, too,
and—in a sort of shock—
he began to sing and dance.
The driver of the truck they were in
asked the commander who was going along
where to put the Jews off
and was told, "A bit further."
There they were told to lie down
and did and, as the lad was lying there,
he heard the noise of bullets whizzing past—
and he, too, was shot.
The bullet came into the nape of his neck
and out through his mouth.

He was still lying there
and the officer who was shooting would pass those he had shot
and, if he saw or heard a sign of life,
would fire a second shot.
In a few minutes after the lad was shot,
he came to
and, when the officer went past, the lad held his breath
so that the officer would think he was dead.

He just kept lying there
and then there was another group of five,
and then a third.
They were all shot.

There was only one soldier guarding the dead
and the lad ran away when he was not looking
and hid in the stable of a non-Jew.
He stayed in the stable two days
and, when the Russians came,
was looking at them through a hole in the wall.
Somebody opened the door, came in and said to him:
"You can go out now. The Russians have come."
And he went out.
A commander of the Russians came and with him a doctor
but the doctor said there was no chance for the lad to live:
he would only live twelve or twenty-four hours at most.
The doctor thought the bullet had broken his spine.
But the bullet had just missed it,
and after thirty-six hours he was still alive.

Some Jews were still alive in the camp
just before the Russians came.
They stayed in an attic
and would not come down when the Germans ordered them to:
they saw what had happened to the others.
So the Germans brought gasoline and set the building on fire.
As far as the lad knew, only three Jews survived
of the thousands brought almost daily to the camp at Chelmno;
and he one of the three.

THE WITNESS

One of the S.S. men caught a woman with a baby in her arms.
She began asking for mercy: if she were shot
the baby should live.
She was near a fence between the ghetto and where Poles lived
and behind the fence were Poles ready to catch the baby
and she was about to hand it over when caught.
The S.S. man took the baby from her arms
and shot her twice,
and then held the baby in his hands.
The mother, bleeding but still alive, crawled up to his feet.
The S.S. man laughed
and tore the baby apart as one would tear a rag.
Just then a stray dog passed
and the S.S. man stooped to pat it
and took a lump of sugar out of his pocket
and gave it to the dog.

[142]

THE WITNESS

Thousands of Germans surrounded the ghetto with machine-guns
and suddenly began to enter it;
those they were to hunt down
were a group of twenty or so young men and women
and between them they had only a revolver, a grenade, two guns
        and some home-made bombs—
which they had to light by matches.
But this handful who were to fight the thousands of Germans
were elated—
smiled at each other, even joked and shook hands

165

because they knew the Germans would pay a price for their lives.
And, after they threw their bombs and hand grenade
and there were dead and wounded among the Germans,
the commander of the Germans ordered his soldiers to collect their
    dead and wounded
and retreat.

But they came back with tanks
and the Molotov bottles of the Jews set fire to a tank.
After that the Germans came in small numbers
searching for the Jews
in cellars and attics, in dugouts and bunkers,
the Germans wearing shoes with rubber soles
and the Jews fighting them
likewise had their feet wrapped in rags
not to be heard.

There were still thousands of Jews in the ghetto—
as many as thirty or fifty thousand—
and at last to clear the ghetto of Jews
the Germans set fire to it:
at first using airplanes
and then by setting fire to building after building
until there was no longer a ghetto
but only block after block of rubble.
Not infrequently Jews stayed in the burning buildings
until, for fear of being burned alive,
they threw mattresses into the street
and jumped.
Some—with bones broken—nevertheless tried to crawl
into blocks of buildings that had not yet been set on fire
or were only partly in flames.
Often the Jews changed their hiding-places during the night
by moving into the ruins of burnt-out buildings

and hid there until found by the patrols.
Many hid in the sewers
and when their voices were heard through the sewer shafts
the men of the S.S. squads, of the police, or engineers
climbed down the shafts to bring out the Jews.
Often they stumbled over Jews already dead;
and it was always necessary to use smoke candles
to drive the Jews out.
But a few Jews went into the sewers
to make their way out of the ghetto,
stooping in the narrow sewers
with the cold dirty water reaching their knees
and even to their lips,
and, if they could get through the Aryan part of the city,
reach the forest
where Jewish guerrillas were still fighting the Germans.

THE NARRATOR

The uprising of the Jews in the Warsaw ghetto began in the spring
of 1943 and lasted about twenty days. Of the thousands of Jews
still in the ghetto when the uprising began perhaps a few hundred
escaped alive. A great number were killed by the blowing up of
their dugouts and the sewers. But, despite the burden on every S.S.
man or German police officer during these actions to drive out the
Jews from Warsaw—where they had once numbered a quarter of a
million—the spirit of the S.S. men and the police officers, it was
noted by one of their superiors, was ''extraordinarily good and
praiseworthy from the first day to the very last.''

TEXTUAL NOTES

The first date following the poem number gives the provenance of the text printed in this edition. (For the titles referred to by the dates, see the Table of Contents.) Other dates indicate the presence of the poem in other books of the author's, with significant textual variants noted. ("1962" refers to *By the Waters of Manhattan: Selected Verse.*) A later printing is identical with the one immediately preceding unless differences are specified.

[1] 1918. 1920: First line omitted. 1927.
[2] 1920. 1918: Line 3: *understanding's*   Line 4: *through a mist*
[3] 1918.
[4] 1918, 1920, 1927.
[5] 1920. 1918: Title: *The Suicide*
[6] 1918. 1920: No stanza break.   Lines 2 and 3 printed as one line.
[7] 1918.
[8] 1918. 1920: Line 1: *mourn you who are killed and* Line 4: line break after *grass* with the fifth line indented and uncapitalized. 1927: line 2 omitted; last two lines recombined in one. 1962.
[9] 1919, 1920, 1927.
[10] 1919. 1920: Title: *Epidemic*   Lines 2 and 3 omitted. 1927, 1962.
[11] 1919. See next note.
[12] 1919. 1920 combines this and the preceding poem in the following:

Like a curtain turning in an open window.

Like a swan effortless
On a lake shaded and still in summer,
Dipping a white neck in the trees' shadow,
Hardly beating the water with golden feet.

Sorrow before her
Was gone like noise from a street,
Snow falling.

1927 condenses further to give:

A white curtain turning in an open window.

A swan, dipping a white neck in the trees' shadow,
Hardly beating the water with golden feet.

Sorrow before her
Was gone like noise from a street,
Snow falling.

[13] 1919, 1920, 1927.
[14] 1927. 1919, 1920: Line 1: *who taught*
[15] 1920, 1927. 1919: Line 1: *grandmother.* followed by stanza
        break. Lines 2 and 3: *Women at windows in still streets /*
        Or reading, the glow on their resting hands.
[16] 1920, 1927.
[17] 1920. 1927.: Lines 1 and 2 omitted. Line 3: *The girls*
[18] 1920. 1927: Title: *August* Line 1: *waves.* Line 2
        omitted. Line 4: *hoofs.* Remainder omitted.
[19] 1920. 1927:

APRIL

The stiff lines of the twigs
Blurred by buds.

[20] 1927. 1920: Line 6: *Within and about*
[21] 1920, 1927.
[22] 1920.
[23] 1920.
[24] 1927. 1921: Line 1: *mother came and sat beside him.*
        "What are you reading? Read Line 2: *"But you wouldn't*
        understand Ma. What's the use?" "Read me a little. What do
        you care? Line 6: *He read to her and she listened gravely,*
        then Line 7: *sheets she* Line 8: *And from*
[25] 1927. 1921: Title: *Sunday Walks* Line 1: line break
        at *dust; / No shade but thin* Line 2: line break at *gloom /*
        Staring . . . at blue Line 3: *slime. Beyond, thickets* Line

4: *tree stretched up, dead.*   Line 5: *A dead*   Line 6:
tide was . . . pool lay on   Line 7: *had thrown*   Line 8:
of tin cans rusted;   Line 9: *crept*   Line 10: *clouds
showed like*

[26] 1927. 1921: Line 4: *to fish mouldy*

[27] 1921, 1927.

[28] 1921. 1927: Line 2: first sentence omitted.

[29] 1921, 1927.

[30] 1927. 1921: Line 2: *his paper of sliced . . . table in back.*
Stanza breaks after lines 2, 5, and 7.

[31] 1927. 1921: Line 2: *through public school*   Line 3:
father engaged her to his . . . face, was short and a little fat.
Line 4: *hates me, he hates me!" / The marriage was elaborate.
Her father was well-to-do and she was the only daughter.*
Line 5: *bought her husband a store among the Italians.*   Line
6: runs on from preceding line. *. . . had saved up money.*
Line 7: *buy at once, he lost patience,*   Line 8: *men's smell
when . . . ditching. He*   Line 10: No line break after
money. Line break after *home.*   Line 11: first sentence is
part of preceding line. *. . . two elder*   Line 12: *her cheeks
. . . help me out . . ."*

[32] 1927. 1921: Line 1: *Walking was too slow, he ran softly
on the balls of his feet. In a month*   Line 3: *was sitting up*
Line 5: *He sat moodily. He thought*   Line 6: *He thought
of noting*   Line 7: *in her eyes to-night.*

[33] 1927. 1921: Line 1: line break at *man. / And on his*
Line 3: *Once she saw his mouth jerk*   Line 4: no quotation
marks.   Line 5: *but could say nothing*   Line 7: *awake
at night*   Line 8: *Next morning she went down to his
store. It*   Line 9: line break at *searched. / For*   Line 10:
prosperous and he had left it, bank . . . all, untouched.
Line 12: line break at *city. / One*   Line 13: line break at
children. / She . . . .

[34] 1921, 1927.

[35] 1927. 1921: Line 3: *had been scrimping from day to day
all her*   Line 4: *When his uncle died, he left him a little
money and just in . . . too weak to walk*

[36] 1927. 1921: Line 3: *near the railroad tracks and the lots*
Line 4: *father had been sick for years; but he was . . . merchandise."*   Line 5: *He gave up his studies and taught in a*

school on the East Side. Line 6: *three, and others . . . most came* Line 8: *day and evening, daily; Sunday he slept all morning and afterwards took a walk.* Line 10: *forty. It had been books and books when a boy, he had to win prizes and a scholarship to keep going. And now so many years in the school.* Line 12: *give up his work to what . . . turn? He felt afraid to break the routine which he had grown used to.*

[37] 1927. 1921: Line 2: *Once the stores were burned* Line 4: *sign on his* Line 7: *do with Mendel?" . . . into Siberia."* Line 9: *took them into the streets to sell.* Line 11: printed as continuation of line 10. *. . . money. His son, the*

[38] 1927. 1921:

His daughter belonged to a club. The club studied modern literature and met, once a month, in each other's house.
When his daughter's turn came she told him that the club would come. That evening thay were to discuss Maeterlinck; but the old man thought that they were coming to meet him.
They were seated at last in the parlor. Embarrassed, she asked them not to begin; her father wanted to speak to them.
The members whispered to each other, "Who is her father?"
"I thank you, young men and women," he said, "for the honor of your visit. I suppose you would like to hear me recite some of my poems." He began to chant.

[39] - [41] 1927. From the new poems of the fifth group.
[42] 1929.
[43] - [64] 1934 (*Jerusalem the Golden*).
[65] 1934 (*In Memoriam: 1933*).
[66] 1936. Parts I and III are in 1962.
[67] 1936. The last six lines of part IV are in 1962.
[68] 1936. 1962 reprints two short extracts.
[69] 1941.
[70] - [78] 1941.
[79] - [88] 1941.
    [80] 1962 prints the first six lines and the last line as two separate poems.
    [87] 1962 prints the last four lines only.

[88]   Part IV (misnumbered III in 1941) of a four-part poem. 1962 prints parts I and II.

[89] - [95]   1959.

[96] - [112]   The author supplied a 1973 typescript of this first (untitled) group of poems in the 1969 book, containing some new poems, some deletions, and some revisions. Texts are 1969, 1973 except as follows:

[99]   1973.

[102]   1973. 1969: lines 2 and 3 combined, as also lines 4 and 5.

[104]   1973.

[107]   1969.

[108]   1973.

[110]   1973. 1969: lines 3 and 4 combined.

[113] - [131]   1969.

[132]   Reprinted from *Midstream*, August-September 1969.

[133] - [142]   1973 typescript supplied by the author.

Printed July 1974 in Santa Barbara & Ann Arbor for the Black Sparrow Press by Noel Young & Edwards Brothers Inc. This edition is published in paper wrappers; there are 250 copies numbered & signed by the poet; & 26 lettered copies handbound in boards by Earle Gray each with a holograph poem by Charles Reznikoff.

Charles Reznikoff was born in a Jewish ghetto in Brooklyn in 1894. His parents were immigrants from Russia. He was graduated from the Brooklyn Boys' High School when not quite sixteen, spent a year at the new School of Journalism of the University of Missouri (1910-1911), and entered the law school of New York University in 1912. Admitted to the bar of the State of New York in 1916, he practiced only briefly. The United States had entered the First World War and in 1918 he was admitted to the officers' training camp at Columbia University, but before he received any training the war was over. His parents were then in business as manufacturers of hats and, for a while, he was a salesman for them, selling to jobbers and large department stores. In 1928, he went to work writing law for the firm publishing *Corpus Juris*, an encyclopedia of law for lawyers. Later, he worked in Hollywood for about three years for a friend who was then a producer for Paramount Pictures. After that, he made his living by freelance writing, research, translating, and editing. In 1962, New Directions published a selection of his verse, *By the Waters of Manhattan*. He was awarded the Jewish Book Council of America's award for English poetry in 1963 and in 1971 the Morton Dauwen Zabel Award for Poetry by the National Institute of Arts and Letters.

He was married in 1930 to Marie Syrkin, now Professor Emeritus of Humanities, Brandeis University.